THE LIVING TRADITIONS OF OLD KYOTO

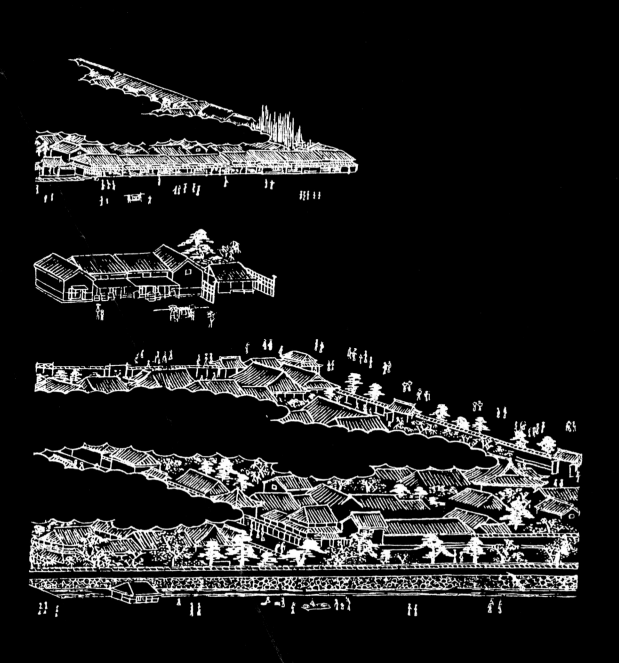

OLD KYOTO

THE LIVING TRADITIONS OF

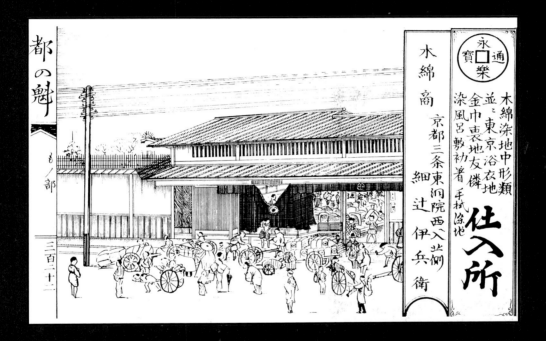

Diane Durston
Lucy Birmingham Fujii

Donald Richie

KODANSHA INTERNATIONAL

TOKYO • NEW YORK • LONDON

This book is dedicated to the townspeople, the craftsmen, and the quiet old wooden neighborhoods that keep the traditions of Kyoto alive. May their warmth and humanity not be lost to the heartless modern development that threatens to destroy Kyoto and so many of the other great historic cities of the world. —D. D.

This special hard-bound edition of
Old Kyoto, with some new material, is published in celebration of
the 1200th anniversary of the founding of
the City of Kyoto in 794.

Old Kyoto was first published in paperback in a
different format by Kodansha International in 1986.

Additional photography courtesy of Gekkeikan and Shoyeido.

Distributed in the United States by
Kodansha America, Inc., 114 Fifth Avenue, New York, New York 10011,
and in the United Kingdom and continental Europe by
Kodansha Europe Ltd., 95 Aldwych, London WC2B 4JF.

Published by Kodansha International Ltd., 17–14 Otowa
1-chome, Bunkyo-ku, Tokyo 112, and Kodansha America, Inc.
Copyright © 1986 and 1994 by Diane Durston, Lucy Birmingham Fujii, and Kodansha International.
All rights reserved. Printed in China.
First edition, 1994.
10 9 8 7 6 5 4 3 2 1
97 96 95 94
ISBN 4–7700–1870–3

LIBRARY OF CONGRESS CATALOGUING-IN-PUBLICATION DATA
Durston, Diane.
The living traditions of old Kyoto/Diane Durston:
photography by Lucy Birmingham Fujii: foreword by Donald Richie.
Includes bibliographical references and index.
1. Kyoto (Japan)—Guidebooks. I. Birmingham, Lucy.
II. Title.
DS897. K83D86 1994 915.2' 18640449—dc20 94–15413 CIP

CONTENTS

FOREWORD   *by Donald Richie*   7

BEGINNINGS   9

KYOTO CRAFTS   11

    Purveyors to the Imperial Household
    Religious Reflections
    The Illustrious Influence of Tea
    Reflections from the Floating World
    Objects of Everyday Use

KYOTO KITCHENS   14

RESTAURANTS & INNS   16

    Ryokan

THE LIVING TRADITIONS—
PEOPLE, PLACES, AND LEGENDS

    I. KYOTO CRAFTS   20

    II. KYOTO KITCHENS   46

    III. RESTAURANTS AND INNS   64

ON KYOTO

History   94

    Raku-chu, Raku-gai—Kyoto's Quarters   101

    Map of Kyoto   105

    Words for Shopkeepers to Live By   106

    Kyoto Dialect—The Gentler Tones of the Ancient Capitol   107

    List of Shops   108

    Suggested Reading List   110

Acknowledgments   111

FOREWORD

by Donald Richie

KYOTO—a fact well publicized—is very special. It holds the imperial past and the cultural best—temples, gardens, cuisine, kimono, crafts.

What is not generally recalled is that Kyoto is what it is because, almost alone among Japanese cities, it was not bombed, remaining untouched during World War II. Thus the old capital looks as all Japan might have, had it not been destroyed.

This being so, Kyoto—or at least parts of it—is still made of wood. It is the only city in Japan, perhaps in the world, so made. To walk the back streets of the old capital is to stroll in a carpentered forest.

Thus Kyoto is more than the official "traditional Japan" one reads about in ordinary guidebooks and takes guided tours to see; it is also these warrens of backstreets with their inns and restaurants and shops, the buildings still made of wood and stone and tile.

As we walk these streets we see the grain, the hue, the texture of wood, watch its changing color, feel its warmth, sense nature. If you half close your eyes and look at these streets you will see how natural they are—the varied textures, the different shapes, the lines of roofs, all natural, all organic, as though growing there.

Here, too, the last of the urban natural. Elsewhere, still, rice paddies harmonize and contrast with the valleys and the hills. The very materials—straw, wood, plaster, paper—are natural; when the dyed cloth was washed in the stream it delineated the current, emphasized the banks, seemed a part of the water itself.

And so even now there are back-street corners in Kyoto where a harmonious accommodation is made between what man has built and what he found—the line of a tree reflected in the line of a pillar; the grain of the rock, the grain of the stone wall.

Even now that concrete is cheaper than stone, metal is cheaper than wood, and plastic is cheaper than anything, the warrens of old buildings—shops, inns, eateries—have no pretensions, do not aspire to become monuments. They can never become a part of the official traditional Kyoto. They are still in use. People live in these old buildings, work in them, always have.

The blank, anonymous postwar look of most Japanese cities is due not only to their having been destroyed by war. They are also being destroyed by the high price of land, the need for larger and more efficient buildings, the price of building materials and the necessity of building with cheap prefab modules, by the national preoccupation with making money.

Indeed, even sections of Kyoto look like Osaka or Nagoya, and in time the resemblance will be closer still. None of the great sights will go—this or that place, that pavilion or this. There may well be some who would prefer a useful modern apartment block to a useless ancient temple, no matter how famous, but the official attitude is against them. The Kyoto city government would never permit this.

But there is no one to speak for these old-fashioned streets where the possibly dangerous wooden buildings are so inefficiently occupying valuable land.

Consequently, some of the finest environments, the ones that speak most truly of living Kyoto—these will vanish. This part of the living fabric of tradition will disappear. "Old Kyoto" will, of course, survive—it is, after all, a city on display where all, Japanese and foreigner alike, come as they would to an exposition.

But traces of the quiet, traditional back streets of Kyoto will not vanish. One of these is the book you are holding. Here the look, the feel, the smell, the tastes of real traditional Kyoto have been preserved.

In her sixteen years in Kyoto, Diane Durston has lived with this true, living tradition. With affection and understanding she now gives it to us, the only account of these streets and their inns and shops and places to eat and to drink.

More than any other book it captures with care, precision, and love those qualities which make the real Kyoto what it still remains.

BEGINNINGS

DUSK SETTLES over the back streets, tucking in the rows of old wooden houses for another peaceful night's sleep. The glow of sunset deepens and hangs between the sagging tile rooftops, telephone lines, and pine branches silhouetted against an indigo sky. Someone's grandfather, bucket and washrag under one arm, clacks down the alley in wooden *geta* on the way to the public bath. The cackle of old women gossiping in doorways echoes in the quiet night air. An old man in white gauze pajamas squats on his doorstep amid a circle of impatient children begging him to light another sparkler to celebrate an ordinary summer's night.

One of the only shops left open on the street is the corner saké shop, where a boisterous caucus of day laborers and pensioners wash down the day's grievances with a cold bottle of beer. The reassuring whir of an electric fan and the shopkeeper's amazing skills of arbitration temper the injustices of eight hours in the relentless Kyoto heat. "*Oideyasu!*" she calls out in Kyoto dialect, welcoming another weary pilgrim into the fold.

The bathhouse is still open, and its entryway curtains wave enticingly at sweltering neighbors with promises of relief. The noodle shop two doors down feeds the last of the day's ravenous boarding-house students, who sit slurping noodles with the cook in front of the TV set, kibitzing the outcome of the ball game.

The vegetable stand, the tofu shop, and the flower vendor have all closed down for the night. So have the knife sharpener, the seal carver, and the lacquerer—their electric fans the only ones working overtime tonight. An hour past supper and the smell of grilled fish still clings to the air. Lights go on behind the latticed paper windows of the houses, making them glow like a corridor of two-story wooden lanterns in the deepening twilight. A temple bell tolls the passage of another day. The local cop bicycles past on his evening rounds, humming; trouble is still a surprise in old Kyoto neighborhoods like these.

If it weren't for the surveyor's stakes on the vacant lot down the street, the year could as easily be 1884 as 1994. Within two weeks a four-story concrete apartment building will wedge its way between the gray-tile rooftops of these "bedrooms of eels," the local nickname for the elongated wood-frame houses whose narrow facades line the streets of the city. This latest modern addition to the old neighborhood, though a disappointment to some, at least is no longer a surprise.

The old wooden buildings, the homes of craftsmen and merchants whose shop fronts open right onto the streets, are disappearing one by one, extracted hygienically like aching teeth, leaving cavities in the landscape and the heart of the ancient city. Made simply of wood, clay, and sand, they are easily demolished, gone within hours on any hot Kyoto afternoon. But with them goes much of the history and charm of this twelve-hundred-year-old city. The old shops and houses gave shelter to a different world. A poorer world, at least economically—kept down by an oppressive class system, dominated by a long line of tyrants—but one in which the common people learned, if only out of sheer necessity, how to live peacefully in cramped quarters, how to turn disaster into progress and poverty into an aesthetic ideal. During ages in which the aristocrats sank in their own decadence and the samurai fought their way to destruction, it was the common people of Kyoto, the merchants and craftsmen, who kept many of the arts and crafts, customs and traditions of their civilization alive.

The old shops of Kyoto, some of whose families boast over twenty generations in the same trade, continue to house the spirit of the ancient capital, quietly tending the simple businesses of their grandfathers, as if the essence of what they represent were tucked safely away in the family shrine behind the urn that holds his ashes.

Wooden buckets and paper umbrellas are still made in the old shops as they were in the seventeenth century, but the citizens of twentieth-century Kyoto haven't much use for them anymore, preferring the "convenience" of plastic and nylon. Many homes in Japan now have their own baths, and few people still relish the pleasures of a soak in the communal tubs of the city's old-fashioned *sento*, or public baths. *Kyo-ryori*, the exquisite local cuisine, now competes with

German delicatessens and French cafes for customers among Kyoto's increasingly cosmopolitan populace.

No one begrudges the improvements in the quality of life that the last century has brought to Japan—modern transportation, better medical care, more of the luxuries once reserved for the upper classes. But a sigh escapes at times, bemoaning the inevitable loss of old-world charm.

Down Kyoto's narrow, anonymous back streets there are still many glimpses of an elegant past. The luster of a hand-painted vermilion lacquer bowl, with an inlaid mother-of-pearl dragonfly, carefully removed from a signed wooden box by a solicitous old shopkeeper's wife … the moment's hesitation before slicing into a sweet bean cake the fragile color and shape of a cherry blossom … the unexpected pleasure of discovering the intricately woven thread pattern that binds the once-common handmade house broom.

The aura of classical Japanese living does still exist in Kyoto. It can be found in the windows of old fan shops, on the doorway curtains of confectioneries, in the tiny gardens of the neighborhood inns. The spirit of the city lives on in the hearts of its traditional shopkeepers. In Kyoto the oldest shops are known as *shinise*, and to qualify for "old" your shop must be at least one hundred years and three generations in the same family—"*hyakunen/sandai.*" There are close to a thousand *shinise* in Kyoto, about four hundred of which date back as far as the Edo period. Any establishment that is younger has not yet proven its mettle—and whether or not the third generation proves successful in the business is the real criterion.

Thousands of tourists, both foreign and Japanese, flock to Kyoto year after year in search of the old spirit. To find it, they take bus tours to famous sights and ancient temples; they visit museums and read pamphlets on religions and warlords; they walk past it without a second glance on their way to catch the train....

The dark facades of the *shinise* of Kyoto all seem alike at first, with their *noren*-curtain veils and absence of signs in English. Even the seasoned traveler (Japanese or foreigner) hesitates to venture further.

But what you'll find inside is often a warmhearted shopkeeper eager to be at your service. My hope is that this book will help you to find what you're looking for in Kyoto, help you to locate the heart of the city.

The back streets, the out-of-the-way corners of the city, explored on foot on your own, reveal its character more assuredly than the gilded palaces of its long-departed warlords and emperors. In a city like Kyoto with a long history of political turmoil and change, it is the everyday people who have borne the responsibility of preserving what is of value in traditional customs and crafts, of handing down the essence of what was good in the past.

The traditional shopkeepers of Kyoto have taken great pains to maintain the old wooden buildings with their sagging beams and sinking stone floors. They insist on making the same fine products with the best materials they can buy, as if they were still Purveyors to the Imperial Household, as many of them once were. They stubbornly cling to old wood-burning stoves, convinced as their grandfathers were that they boil a tastier pot of rice. They shun power tools, knowing nothing can match the character of a surface that has been laboriously polished by hand.

They are aware that the twentieth century has made many of their products passé, and search for ways to show modern customers that the quality of life does not depend entirely on the number of electric appliances on the kitchen counter. They hope their children will take over when they die, but live in the knowledge that, for many of them, their shop's legacy will be buried with them as their sons hurry off to Osaka in search of fashionable office jobs.

The famous temples and manicured villas may define the rarefied soul of feudal Japan, but the old noodle shops and inns, the teahouses and bucket makers, are the marrow of its bones. Walk around Kyoto; part the curtains of the old shops; step inside…"*Oideyasu!*"

Diane Durston
Kyoto

KYOTO CRAFTS

FOR YEARS—centuries, in fact—the rivers of Kyoto flaunted their brilliant Yuzen colors as the long streamers of hand-painted silk gave up their excess dye to their cold, clear waters. In the Gojozaka District near Kiyomizu Temple, the huge climbing kilns puffed and snorted their black smoke into the Kyoto skies, turning the efforts of local potters into gleaming porcelain. The great "Thousand-Armed" Kannon, Goddess of Mercy, and her thousand equally-armed companion images stood watch over rows and rows of open fans that were laid out to dry in the courtyard before her. The constant *kattan-kotton* clanking of thirty thousand looms shook the foundations of the wood-frame houses along the narrow streets of Nishijin, the weaving district, famed for the production of exquisite silk *obi* sashes.

Far to the north, woodsmen carefully trimmed the towering cedar trees, shaving them like the legs of college women, flawlessly preparing them to decorate the homes of the wealthy. Kyoto bustles today as it did in the seventeenth century; the skies and waters are colored now with a different sort of affliction.

The crafts of Kyoto have changed, but they have survived. Baskets are still woven, scrolls mounted, incense prepared with formulas that are still family secrets. Knives and fine carving tools are forged, and O-Shaka-sama is still cast in bronze and gilded here. What has changed is not so much the objects themselves, but the role they play in Japanese society. Today the craftsman decorates where once he filled a daily need. His products that were affordable are costly now, and he himself has become an artist rather than a craftsman. There was no word for "art" in the Japanese language until the nineteenth century.

Doll makers once made figures that were an essential part of annual festivals for children. Though many dolls of this kind are still produced, the festival has lost much of its religious significance. At exhibitions of the work of Kyoto's top contemporary doll makers, the focus is on the show of decorative art and sculpture.

Adjectives like rustic and rough-hewn have no place in the vocabulary of Kyoto crafts; the defining word here is *miyabi*, the elusive element of imperial refinement and elegance that characterizes even the most common of everyday objects produced in the former capital.

Kyoto's crafts evolved out of cultural phenomena that developed over the centuries and can be grouped accordingly. The presence of the Imperial Court in Kyoto; the development of the tea ceremony; the position of the ancient capital as the center of Buddhism in Japan; and the lavish entertainment world of geisha and kabuki were some of the primary factors influencing the extraordinary level of craftsmanship that developed throughout the long history of Kyoto.

Purveyors to the Imperial Household

Ever since the Emperor Kanmu arrived in Kyoto in the eighth century, the strongest influence on Kyoto craftsmen has been the presence of the Imperial Court. From that time on, the privilege of being selected as *kunaicho-goyotashi*—a Purveyor to the Imperial Household—was an honor unparalleled among the craftsmen, merchants, and chefs who were at the exclusive disposal of the court. Throughout the middle ages these select few were given special wooden placards granting them admittance to the Imperial Palace compound. Though the practice was abolished after World War II, many old shopkeepers still proudly keep their original placards as family heirlooms and symbols of the "royal" quality of their traditional products.

Several *kunaicho-goyotashi* shops can be found in the area around the Gosho, the Old Imperial Palace, between Imadegawa and Oike from Kawaramachi to Horikawa.

Among the crafts that developed in accordance with the taste of the Heian court were the finely dyed silk brocades for the twelve-layered *junihitoe* robes worn by ladies-in-waiting; painted and natural-wood folding fans (*sensu*); musical instruments like the *koto* (zither), the *biwa* (lute), the large *taiko* (drum), the *tsuzumi* (hourglass-shaped hand drum), and a variety of flutes (*fue*). Lacquer ware, or *shikki*, was so popular at court that it replaced pottery as the material most commonly used in making serving vessels. One of the aspects of Kyoto cuisine, or *Kyo-ryori*, that adds elegance to the overall sensory experience is the continued use of fine lacquer ware. *Maki-e*, the technique of sprinkling gold or silver dust onto a still-damp lacquer ground, was developed during the Heian period for the exclusive benefit of the Imperial Court.

Religious Reflections

Kyoto has long been the spiritual heart of Japan. Shinto and Buddhism, the two major religions of Japan, have always been centered in the city, and many great monuments to both are located here. The *Gosan* temples (literally, "Five Great Moun-

tains") of Zen, Nanzen-ji, Daitoku-ji, Kennin-ji, Tenryu-ji, and Tofuku-ji, are located in Kyoto. So are a number of powerful shrines: Kitano-jinja, Yoshida-jinja, Himukai-taisha, and Yasaka-jinja. Shrines and temples both represented places of relative stability during times of war in the capital. Merchants and craftsmen conducted regular fairs at the major shrines and temples, which were considered a kind of central gathering place for many of the guilds, offering them protection from the shogunate in exchange for special taxes. This arrangement kept the priests in a position of power.

Craftsmen and merchants built their homes and shops in front of the gates of temples, creating townships called *monzen-machi*. They produced religious articles (*butsugu*), including Buddhist home altars (*butsudan*) constructed of lacquered wood with elaborate gilded carvings and chased metal fittings, and sculpture (*butsuzo*) in carved wood or cast bronze.

Hundreds of small religious objects—like incense burners, (*koro*) and incense (*ko* or *senko*), bronze bells (*kane*) and wooden gongs (*mokugyo*), candles (*rosoku*) and prayer beads (*juzu*)—can still be found in the shops in front of the main gates of both Nishi and Higashi Hongan-ji temples north of Kyoto Station. These two powerful temples are the headquarters of two branches of the powerful Jodo Sect of Buddhism, and worshippers from rural prefectures make frequent pilgrimages here, buying Buddhist articles made by Kyoto craftsmen to take home to their local temples.

In almost every neighborhood, at least one shop makes Shinto household altars (*kamidana*) and the portable shrines (*mikoshi*) used in neighborhood shrine festivals. The smooth, natural finish of a Shinto shrine and its smaller representations epitomizes the Japanese love of simple, unadorned beauty. The fine Japanese traditions of woodwork and joinery that go into the making of these diminutive spirit-houses were handed down by the highly specialized craftsman (*miya-daiku*) who built (and now rebuild) the shrines, temples and teahouses of Japan. Today, these skills are known to only a few. One temple carpenter told me he was booked with more orders for repairs than he could possibly accomplish in his lifetime.

The Illustrious Influence of Tea

One of the strongest and deepest impressions left on the arts and crafts of Kyoto is that of *Sado* (or *Chado*), the Way of Tea, popularly known as the tea ceremony. When tea was first brought to Japan from China by Buddhist priests in the eighth century, it was valued for its medicinal properties and became a permanent item on the list of exotic luxuries reserved for the aristocracy. They imbibed the heady beverage with formal pomp and ceremony, collecting the treasured utensils of the Chinese, and holding lavish tea parties in the court pavilions.

Not until the time of Murata Shuko (1422–1502) did the custom of drinking tea take on the spiritual aspect that gave it a central role in the subsequent development of Japanese culture. Following the teachings of Ikkyu, the legendary Zen priest, Murata developed a concept of tea as a ritual and a discipline for the mind and body, combined with the same aesthetic values promoted by Zen—simplicity, refinement, and restraint. These were qualities that the samurai, or *bushi*, sought as a counter-balance to the decadence and excesses they saw as having brought about the decline of the aristocracy.

The popularity of the tea ceremony stimulated the development of crafts that could not only produce the many specialized utensils that became an aspect of central importance to this ritualized practice, but also meet its unique aesthetic demands for *wabi*, the sensibility of "rustic poverty" sought after by the great tea masters of Kyoto. Sen no Rikyu, tea master and cultural adviser to Hideyoshi in the late sixteenth century, formalized the practice of *wabi-cha*, or *wabi*-style tea, and designed implements in keeping with the aesthetic and spiritual ideals it represented. The first *Raku* tea bowls were made at Rikyu's request by the Korean potter Chojiro, a former roof-tile maker who was awarded the name *Raku* by Hideyoshi in honor of his accomplishments.

The tea bowl (*chawan*) was of primary importance, though bamboo tea whisks (*chasen*), tea scoops (*chashaku*), lacquered tea caddies (*natsume*), fresh-water containers (*mizusashi*), waste-water containers (*kensui*), bamboo ladles (*hishaku*), iron teakettles (*kama*), flower vases (*hana-ire*), and an assortment of other objects all fall under the category of *cha-dogu*, the utensils necessary for the tea ceremony.

Bamboo ware, ceramics, lacquer ware (for the service of *cha-kaiseki*, the meal that accompanies a formal tea ceremony), metalwork, and textiles (both for garments worn by *chajin*, or "tea people," and the latter also used to wrap the precious utensils before they are placed in their wooden storage boxes) all became essential elements in the practice of tea.

Other skills required were the making of special charcoal for heating tea water, the preparation of aromatic woods and subtly blended incense (*ko*) burned before guests arrived, and the production of tatami mats, *shoji* paper windows, and *fusuma* sliding doors—all of which evolved from the tearooms of the shogun Ashikaga Yoshimasa at Ginkaku-ji temple. His Silver Pavilion in the northeast of Kyoto and the tiny four-mat room called the Dojin-sai were the settings for countless tea ceremonies, and created the standard for those that would follow.

The Ashikaga also promoted a solemn form of theater called Noh, which conformed with the Zen principles of economy of expression and restraint admired by the samurai. Many of the masks (*noh-men*) and ornate costumes in silk damask or embroidered silk gauze that were made by craftsmen in the seventeenth and eighteenth centuries for use in the Noh drama are still worn on the stage today.

Reflections from the Floating World

A more down-to-earth, if equally esoteric, influence on the arts and crafts of Kyoto came from the bawdy, nocturnal world of the geisha quarters. The peaceful seventeenth and eighteenth centuries brought prosperity and leisure time to the merchant class, who created their own colorful world of entertainment. Considered vulgar by the upper classes, the "floating world" depicted in *ukiyo-e* woodblock prints of the day depict scenes of willowy courtesans arrayed in exuberantly decorated kimono, draping themselves languidly over their balconies, sighing under the midsummer moon.

The brilliantly dyed and embroidered kimono of the geisha, the elaborate hair ornaments (*kanzashi*) of lacquer, gold, silver, tortoiseshell, and glass; the tall platform *pokkuri geta* of their *maiko* apprentices; the sweeping kimono sashes (*obi*); the oiled paper umbrellas (*wa-gasa*); and a long list of accessories ranging from round *uchiwa* fans to long, slender tobacco pipes (*kiseru*)—all were a part of the romantic world of Gion, the main geisha quarter of Kyoto.

Kabuki was generally considered the theater "of the people," in contrast with the more aristocratic

KYOTO KITCHENS

Noh; its boldly patterned costumes, exotic makeup, and swashbuckling flamboyance provided Kyoto craftsmen with constant challenges in pattern design and color composition.

Threatened by the economic prowess of the rising merchant class, the Tokugawa shogunate forbid shop owners to wear the costly silk brocades that were the pride of the upper classes. Unwilling to be so easily dismissed, the merchants urged dyers to match the extravagance of elaborate weaves with dyeing techniques that would produce an equally sumptuous effect. *Yuzen*, the paste-resist technique of fabric dyeing invented by Miyazaki Yuzen, a former fan painter, was developed during this era, achieving finely lined results that must have aggravated the floundering lawmakers beyond words.

Objects for Everyday

To the rich and powerful of every culture may go the finest of its arts and crafts, but the refinement and skillfulness of the most common household objects in Kyoto are a clue to the level of craftsmanship achieved by society as a whole. A simple hand-cut, hand-polished boxwood comb (*tsuge-kushi*)—something no bride would be without in old Kyoto—is an object of delicate beauty. Buckets (*oke, taru*) with staves carefully planed to fit the proper angle and then joined with tiny bamboo pegs, are as suitable for displaying on a shelf as for carrying sushi. The same goes for the wooden foot-wear (*geta*) that is hand-carved from a single block of paulownia.

The everyday necessities of life for the common people of Kyoto—butcher knives (*hocho*), sewing needles (*hari*), roof tiles (*kawara*), workmen's coats (*hanten, happi*), shop curtains (*noren*), farmers' trousers (*monpe*), chests of drawers (*tansu*), signature seals (*hanko*), paper lanterns (*bonbori, chochin*)—all possess an undeniable sense of gentility not ordinarily associated with things so ordinary. For instance, you don't know the pleasure a pair of socks can bring until you've been custom-fitted for a dazzling white pair of cotton *tabi* that button neatly at the ankle.

DRIED BEANS, sea urchin jelly, cod roe, fish paste, chrysanthemums (both to arrange and to eat), seaweed, live eels, raw oysters, flakes of dried bonita for making soup, rice cakes, grilled squid… What more could you ask? The aromas of fresh roasted tea, ovens steaming with hot bean cakes, and skewered fish dripping with soy sauce over a charcoal grill (this latter pleasure admittedly reserved for Orientally-adjusted noses). The sounds of shopkeepers calling out a hearty "*Irasshai*" of welcome, and fishmongers touting the day's catch in boisterous tones: "*Oishii yo!*" ("Delicious!"). Finally, a riot of color—shiny red apples stacked in perfect pyramids beside equally impeccable towers of persimmons, green vegetables (some familiar, and others, like fern fronds, more obscure), and live shrimp, crabs, abalone, and more varieties of fish than you knew existed. Sprinkle in a few old shops selling knives and cookware, *geta* clogs, or pottery bowls and you have the street markets and food shops of old Kyoto—one for every neighborhood, and plenty to go around.

Since the middle ages, Nishiki, still the city's liveliest street market, has been the site of a public market selling fish, produce, and saké. It was destroyed in the Onin War (1467–77), but was rebuilt in the late 1500s and has operated continuously as a market-place since. Today the shopkeepers of Nishiki still follow the custom of careful specialization observed by their early merchant ancestors. Shops selling freshwater fish don't deal in fish from the sea. Egg shops sell eggs, but no chicken. Some shops sell only shellfish, while others specialize in blowfish or eel. This division dates back to the guilds established in Kyoto in the thirteenth century for mutual protection and profit during the turbulent times. By the sixteenth century, these distinctions had evolved into a strict system of government favoritism that gave particular merchants absolute monopolies on the goods they sold, including the right to pass on their trade to their descendants in exchange for taxes.

The merchants of Nishiki still work in cooperation with one another, and though competition exists, the almost endless variety of specialty items in the Japanese diet and the similarly endless throngs of eager customers—each of which patronizes the same shop her grandmother did—make for a harmonious atmosphere in the old marketplaces of Kyoto.

Most of the shops are open by mid-morning, which is the hour to find many of Kyoto's most lauded chefs shopping for the special foods they need to prepare the elaborate *kaiseki* meals. In the afternoon, the local housewives converge on the

market; Nishiki is always crowded by 3 p.m. Working people stop by on their way home, and most shops stay open until about 7 p.m.

Nishiki is one block north of Shijo-dori and runs from Teramachi-dori on the east to Takakura-dori on the west. It is four hundred meters long and houses the 141 shops that line the narrow market street. Look for Aritsugu, a cutlery and traditional kitchenware shop, on Nishiki's north side, one block west of Teramachi. Further east, on the corner of Fuyacho-dori, is Jintora, a sweet shop that specializes in *kodai-gashi*, or old-style sweets. Over a dozen wooden cases with glass lids hold sweets of different shapes, each molded and colored in designs appropriate to the season—pine needles, maple leaves, plum blossoms, and hundreds more. About halfway between Fuyacho and Tominokoji, you'll find

Tsunayoshi, a saké shop selling *ji-zaké*, saké made in small villages all over Japan.

But Nishiki is not the only market street in Kyoto. Every neighborhood has its own *shoten-gai*, to which housewives still dedicated to shopping daily for just enough food for the evening's meal, come each afternoon. shopping bag in hand.

Kyoto cuisine is noted for its delicate seasoning, and for the priority it places on using the finest ingredients available only in season. Located at least a day's walk from the sea, it also has a long tradition of pickling and salt-curing fish. For Japanese visiting from other regions, *Kyo-tsukemono* (Kyoto-style pickled vegetables) and *Kyo-gashi* (Kyoto-style sweets) are favorite souvenirs. The city is home to many Buddhist temples, and some of its most basic specialty foods, such as tofu (bean curd), *fu* (wheat gluten dumplings) and *yuba* (soy milk skimmings) were originally devised as ways of supplementing protein in the vegetarian diet of Buddhist monks.

The influence of the Way of Tea is evident in the abundance of shops specializing in producing sweets. No neighborhood in Kyoto is without a traditional sweet shop. Many of these have remained unchanged, making bean cakes from the same recipe, in the same old shops, and even for the same dedicated families of customers, for centuries.

RESTAURANTS & INNS

Western food—
Every damn plate
is round.
Anonymous modern *senryu* (satirical poem)

A LENGTH OF FRESHLY split green bamboo, a three-layered ceramic serving dish in the shape of a gourd, a red and black lacquered tray carved in the shape of a flower and painted delicately in gold with the single bough of a cherry tree in full bloom… Japanese food is never boring.

Kyoto, as the old imperial capital, was also the birthplace of *kaiseki*, the exquisite formal cuisine that doesn't forget the other four senses. Environment is the first consideration. Seated on *zabuton* cushions in a private tatami-mat room overlooking a meticulously groomed garden with only the sound of water trickling from the stone basin just outside to accent the silence…you are ready to begin.

The door slides open and a lady in kimono (sometimes jolly, more often demure) enters to hand you a hot towel to wipe your hands—a simple but civilized custom that soon becomes hard to live without.

A *kaiseki* meal is served in at least seven courses, each prepared in a different manner and from ingredients appropriate to the season. The range of flavors, from sweet to sour, and salty to mild, is subtly planned so that each succeeding flavor will complement the last. Ingredients are only used at the peak of their season, and accents of seasonal color—a maple leaf in autumn or sprig of plum blossoms in spring—inevitably appear. One particularly "Kyoto" touch is that only the lightest seasoning is added. Kyoto restauranteurs believe that the natural flavors of fine ingredients speak for themselves.

A typical course might include appetizers (*zensai*), raw fish (*otsukuri*), a seafood and vegetable "salad" (*aemono*), one or more soups (*suimono* or *shirumono*), simmered foods (*ni-mono*), steamed dishes (*mushimono*), broiled or grilled foods (*yakimono*), deep-fried tidbits (*agemono*), vinegared "salad" (*sunomono*), rice (*gohan*), pickles (*tsukemono*), and perhaps a bowl of fruit for dessert. The combinations are endless and left to the chef's

discernment, though a formal order of dishes and ingredients appears in the case of *cha-kaiseki*, which is the meal that accompanies a tea ceremony, or served in restaurants specializing in this cuisine. *Cha* means tea; *kaiseki*, in this case written with characters that mean "a stone in the folds of a kimono," refers to the old Zen practice of sending priests to bed with nothing but a hot stone tucked into their kimono to keep their bellies warm. A *cha-kaiseki* meal served in "modest portions" is intended to be just enough to do the same, while complementing the flavor of thick green tea.

The *kaiseki* served in other restaurants is written with characters meaning "banquet." This style evolved from the saké parties at teahouses that became popular in the nineteenth century and often required the services of geisha.

Whichever the style, part of the magic of a *kaiseki* meal for the novice is having no idea what you are eating, much less what comes next. The joy is in discovery. The possibilities are so vast that warlords and wealthy merchants of the Edo period—experts in the realm of the senses—even made a game of guessing which foods they had been presented during an evening's entertainment and drinking. A spirit of adventure is a prerequisite; the reward is a sensory experience you will not soon forget.

A *kaiseki* meal in one of the finest *ryotei*, as the houses of Kyoto's haute cuisine are known, can be very expensive. Considering the long hours involved in making such a wide variety of delicate dishes and the often priceless, heirloom ceramics and lacquer ware on which the meal is served, however, you understand that you are paying for an experience once the sole right of royalty. The best of Kyoto's restaurants make it a rule never to serve a guest the same meal twice, even if he or she dines there more than once within the same season. The proprietress takes careful note of each guest's likes and dislikes, catering to the patron's every whim in order to ensure that every meal is memorable.

One retired restaurant owner confided to me that anything over a moderate price pays for the fine dishware on which the meal is served and the treasured appointments—hanging scrolls by famous calligraphers and flower vases centuries old—of the private room. The connoisseur (*tsu*) of Kyoto cuisine looks forward, with each visit, to being able to name the craftsman and date the priceless serving dishes that appear in the course of a meal.

Much less expensive options do exist, and one marvelous alternative is the elaborate box lunch *Kyo-bento* served at many of the best places for a fraction of the cost. Usually served only during the day, the *o-bento* provides an excellent sampler of the cuisine offered at each restaurant, though at times you must forego the private room and the luxury of spending the requisite minimum of two hours over a full-course *kaiseki* meal.

Although most people think only of *kaiseki* when *Kyo-ryori* is mentioned, the essential elements of an old-fashioned Kyoto family-style meal were salted fish and pickled vegetables. Located far from the nearest sea, the people of Kyoto found it necessary to invent a thousand ways of preparing and preserving both these basic foodstuffs. *Kyo-tsukemono*, the pickled vegetables which are served with rice, are famous throughout Japan, and one of the first souvenirs Japanese visiting from other districts are likely to buy.

Shojin ryori, the vegetarian food served in Buddhist temples, was developed in Kyoto from its prototype, *fucha ryori*, brought by priests from China. Both the adapted and the original, imported styles are still served for lunch in many of Kyoto's Buddhist temples. Local specialties like *yuba* (skimmed soybean milk), *nama-fu* (a wheat-flour dumpling), and an assortment of tofu (bean curd) dishes are all a part of *shojin ryori*. These high pro-tein, low-calorie foods are served in a variety of unusual dishes that make healthy vegetarian-style dining a very pleasurable experience in Kyoto.

Though sushi and sukiyaki are popular in the West, many people hesitate to try Japan's more exotic fare, because of cultural misgivings about squid, fish roe, and sea urchin. But skipping an opportunity to try *Kyo-ryori* night is like going to New York and failing to visit a delicatessen. I recommend trying each dish first and asking questions later. You'd be surprised how good a sea urchin can taste.

Ryokan

Stone walkways lead off the narrow side streets to one-or two-story tile-roofed inns in which hand-polished wooden corridors twist and turn past peaceful interior gardens to your room. Tatami mats,

an alcove (*tokonoma*) in which a bamboo basket of fresh flowers was placed hours earlier in anticipation of your arrival, a hanging scroll (that has been in the family for generations), a small lacquered writing box, and a closet full of thickly quilted *futon* bedding... A combination of small things surrounds you with comfort and the sense of being a true guest. Acclaimed internationally for their warm hospitality, fine service, and excellent cuisine, Kyoto's traditional inns offer a chance to experience first-hand the amenities once reserved for noblemen and feudal lords.

A night in a traditional Japanese inn, or *ryokan*, is not an experience to be missed, no matter how much easier it may sound to seek refuge in one of the major hotels. A hotel is a hotel, whether in St. Louis or St. Moritz, but a *ryokan* is a sample of traditional Japanese living at its finest. For this singular pleasure, however, there are certain minor difficulties that must first be surmounted, and this is where the real cultural adventure begins.

Any Japanese innkeeper will have a number of humorous "foreigner at the inn" tales to tell. The old stand-by relates the story of the American who walked into the immaculate tatami-mat room at the *ryokan* to find the maid, who had just arrived with a fresh pot of tea, staring down at his feet in horror. After what seemed an eternity of shocked silence, came the stark realization that he was still wearing the toilet slippers! There are a few classic intricacies to "*ryokan* life" that, once unfolded, could put an end to an entire school of contemporary Japanese innkeeper humor. A few suggestions may help:

Take off your shoes and relax. If you spend any amount of time at all in Japan, this becomes a way of life. Shoes are considered dirty and should always be left at the door. This seems reasonable enough—until you carry the principle to the matter of slippers.

Slippers fall into two basic categories—corridor slippers and toilet slippers—and never the twain shall meet. When you take off your shoes in the entryway to a traditional home, restaurant, or inn, you will be given a pair of slippers in which to walk down the wooden corridor to your room. Take them off before you step onto tatami. Stockinged feet are preferable to bare feet in Japan, but even bare feet are better than slippers on tatami. Put your slippers back on when you leave your room to shuffle down the hall to the toilet, take them

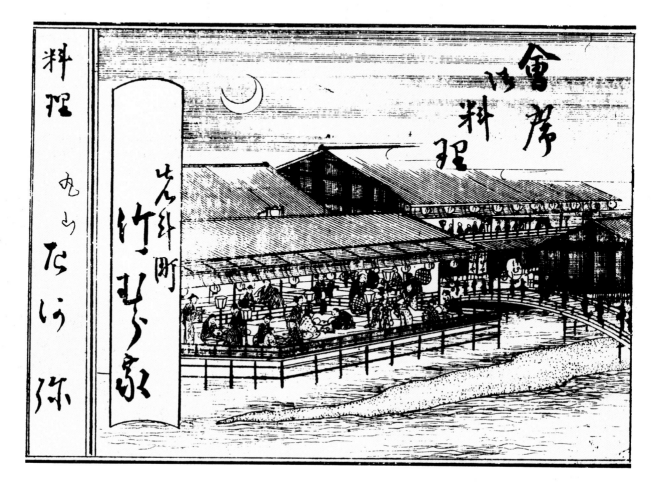

each *ryokan*, it doesn't mean that everyone jumps in at once. There is usually one for men and another for women, or separate bathing times for the two sexes. Many *ryokan* call guests to the bath one family at a time, so you have all the privacy you like. A few of the most expensive inns have private baths in every room to accommodate their more modest guests, but there is a fine custom in Japan called *hadaka no tsuki-ai*, or "naked friendship," which refers to the great ice-breaking effect of sharing a bath with a roomful of strangers. You meet the nicest people, and have an opportunity to make new friends from whom you have no secrets.

By the way, bills at Japanese inns are calculated per person rather than per room. Nowadays many of the old inns do permit guests to stay overnight *shokuji nashi* (without meals), which often brings the price down to a less daunting sum. It is, however, true that many of the finest inns in Kyoto are noted for their excellent cuisine, and passing up a chance to sample it, in the decadent privacy of your own room, can be a definite loss when you consider that comparable meals elsewhere in town can cost just as much.

None of this matters in the least when you wake up in the morning, snuggled inside a thick *futon*, to watch the snow fall in the garden just outside your room. In a few moments, the maid will arrive with the breakfast tray, bowing politely as she begs your pardon for disturbing an elegant night's sleep.

off, and step into the wooden slippers you'll find just inside the restroom door. The trick is remembering to reverse the process on your way back to your room.

Take a bath before you take a bath. In other words, bathtubs in Japan are for soaking, not for washing, which is done seated on a little stool before you get in. Soap up, rinse off, and then step into the tub which is usually torrid enough to make you think that someone has mistakenly left the hot water running. This is a carry-over from the days when each two-story Japanese home was heated by a single charcoal hibachi and the heat you absorbed from the bath was intended to keep you warm long enough to get inside your *futon* and go to sleep before frostbite set in. Modern gas heaters are taken for granted in many homes today, but this old custom —like many others—hangs on.

Don't let the term "communal bath" frighten you. Though there is generally only one bath in

SECTION 1

CRAFT SHOPS

AIZEN KOBO	indigo textiles
HIRATA	blinds
TSUJITA	combs
KAGOSHIN	bamboo
AIZAWA BAISEN-AN	fans
MORITA WAGAMI	handmade paper
NAITO	brooms and brushes
NAKANISHI TOKU SHOTEN	antique dolls
SAIUNDO	Japanese-painting supplies
NISHIHARU	woodblock prints
TARUDEN	buckets
YAMATO MINGEI-TEN	folk art
SHOYEIDO	incense

愛染工房

AIZEN KOBO
indigo textiles

Down a narrow back street in Nishijin, the heart of the textile district in Kyoto, stands the house of an old kimono-sash (*obi*) weaving family established over a century ago. Today, as Aizen Kobo, they specialize in indigo dyeing, or *ai-zome*, a traditional folk technique most often found in remote areas of the Japanese countryside. A century ago, the Utsuki family were masters of *tsuzure-ori*, the tedious "fingernail weaving" technique that produces the intricate tapestry weave seen in the finest Kyoto-style *obi*, often laced with threads of silver and gold. The second-generation weaver in the family, the late Shozo Utsuki, wove *nishiki* brocades, also for *obi*, but with the decline in popularity of kimono for everyday wear there was less call for the costly *obi*, and he was faced with a dilemma that has become a fact of life for traditional craftsmen all over Japan.

It was then that Shozo had the good fortune to join with other craftsmen to form the Mingei

(Folk Art) Movement. Kanjiro Kawai, renowned Kyoto potter and one of the leaders of the group, persuaded Shozo to learn the old folk ways of indigo dyeing and *sashiko* embroidery, crafts that were then considered lowbrow and seemed destined to become extinct. Kawai saw that the beauty of natural indigo dye and the quality of simple handwoven, handmade garments would one day again come into its own. Fortunately, Shozo agreed and began to change the complex production methods of his *obi* business to the simple folk-methods of weaving cotton and linen. He insisted on using only the purest natural dyes and the highest-quality fabrics.

When Shozo changed over from making extravagant silk *obi* to making simple folk wear, the famous novelist Jun'ichiro Tanizaki gave the shop a new name to fit its new way of life. The *ai* in "Aizen Kobo" is a play on words, meaning both love and indigo. *Kobo* means dye house. Kanjiro Kawai himself did the calligraphy for the solid zelkova shop sign, which was carved by Tatsuaki Kuroda (later to be

designated one of Japan's Living National Treasures).

Today the shop is run by Shozo's son, Ken'ichi Utsuki, who carries on his father's work. Aizen Kobo is one of the only places in Kyoto where handwoven, hand-dyed, and hand-embroidered garments and fabrics of *hon-ai*, or "real" indigo, can be found.

The shop deals in a wide variety of indigo-dyed textiles off the bolt, including *kasuri* (ikat) and *shima* (stripes) woven in cotton; *shibori* (tie-dyeing) in cotton and silk; and *katazome* (stencil-dyeing) on cotton or linen. Indigo-dyed ramie, a linen-like fiber that becomes feather soft with use, is also available by the meter.

One of the most popular garments at Aizen Kobo is the *samu-e*, a loose-fitting, two-piece garment worn by Zen priests and local craftsmen. Dyed with *hon-ai*, they look and feel better after five years of regular wear than they do the day you first put them on. The color fades gracefully and the durable fabric becomes softer and softer. When *sashiko* embroidery, a farmers' technique of stitching layers of cotton

together to make the garment stronger, is also used, the result is a *samu-e* that is nearly indestructible.

The much photographed and beautifully restored building that houses Aizen Kobo was built in the Meiji period. It is one of the few in the Nishijin area that have been kept in their original condition and is considered a cultural asset.

Many of the beautiful doorway curtains (*noren*) you see hanging outside traditional Kyoto shops were made at Aizen Kobo. It also has a limited selection of antique textiles, including several *tsutsugaki* dyed coverlets of the kind once used to cover wedding trunks for delivery to the bride's new home, and Aizen Kobo's resident weaver, Hiroshi Matsuguchi, has begun to revive the *tsutsugaki* resist-paste dyeing technique, a folk tradition that has nearly died out in Japan in recent years. By reviving folk traditions, the people at Aizen Kobo have found a "new" old medium in which to survive the transition to modern times.

HIRATA
blinds

Just after sunset, Gion, the old geisha quarter, begins to stir with Kyoto's own special brand of night life— *maiko* in their trailing *obi* sashes, kitchen maids scurrying back to their inns with last-minute purchases for dinner, businessmen on expense accounts gathering a second wind for a night of serious drinking at their favorite club. *Sudare* blinds flapping gently in the breeze on the windows of teahouses that line the old stone canal in Gion are a symbol of the geisha world they half conceal.

Particularly in the Shinbashi district, one of the few official historic preservation districts in Kyoto, the *sudare* has become an essential element in the facades of the buildings.

A block south of Shinbashi on Nawate-dori is a shop that makes many of the famous *sudare* of Gion. Hirata has been making bamboo and reed blinds for two hundred years, but like other craftsmen his age, Yoshio Hirata, a seventh-generation screen-maker, had no chance to learn his trade from his father. Hirata-san was twelve years old when World War II broke out and his father was drafted into the Imperial Army. Kyoto lost many of its finest craftsmen to the war, and Hirata-san's father was one of them. The day before the surrender was declared, their shop building was torn down in the interests of the war effort, without the head of the household present to defend it. Hirata-san learned his trade after the war from craftsmen who, unlike his father, returned home safely.

Sudare blinds were once a necessary part of everyday life in Kyoto, where summers are hot and humid and mosquitoes a constant problem. *Sudare* allowed the paper *shoji* windows to be removed in summertime for ventilation while still shading the rooms from the heat of the sun. They also afforded a bit of privacy along crowded streets with houses built right up to the edges. With the introduction of aluminum sash windows and metal screens after the war, *sudare* became a luxury item used primarily for decorative purposes.

There are several different kinds of *sudare* classified according to use and materials. The heavier, outdoor type are called *hi-oke sudare*. They come in a variety of materials including *take* (bamboo), *yoshi* (a hollow, jointed, yellowish reed), *gama* (a solid, beige reed without joints), and *hagi* (the dark-brown branches of a shrub).

Sudare for interior use in tearooms and as room dividers during the summer months are called *zashiki sudare*, and have a fabric border in brocade or linen. The reeds of *zashiki sudare* are usually of bamboo, though more finely split than those for

exterior use. Often, when the material used is jointed, like bamboo, the joints are laid out to create a pattern on the finished blind—the more intricate the design, the more costly they become.

A third type of blind is called *misu*, the very finest variety, formerly used to hide the emperor from the eyes of the public. Now they are used mainly in temples or shrines for formal occasions. As with many of the accoutrements of court life, the making of *misu* was regulated by protocol, which determined every detail—the number of reeds in each, the type of patterns their joints formed, and the kind of brocade used to border them.

Hirata makes blinds to fit any space required, although at busy times customers can expect to wait a month or more. If you choose the appropriate trim from fabric samples in Hirata-san's catalog, a standard-size order can usually be filled in a couple of days. He makes each blind himself at the back of his shop on a machine that can be seen from the counter. An average *sudare* is about a yard and a half long by a little over a yard wide.

JUSAN-YA
combs

A simple comb can be a work of art—a wonder, when you consider that the man who sits on the floor before his workbench day after day, filing each tooth by hand, has lived in a world of plastic since his birth. Pocket combs are disposable items in a plastic world; who takes the time or trouble to fuss with a handmade wooden comb that could easily be lost and just as easily replaced with celluloid for a fraction of the cost?

Michikazu Takeuchi does—and has for sixty years. He is a sixth-generation maker of boxwood combs (*tsuge-kushi*). He says it takes over forty years to make a proper comb—thus giving much of the credit to the tree itself, together with the decade allowed for the wood to be correctly stored and dried. In Japan, most woodcraftsmen work from a stock of wood purchased by the previous generation, so that it will have been properly dried long enough in advance. After the tree is felled, a minimum of ten years is required for the drying process. The wood is cut into wedges and fumigated with smoke from its own sawdust to ensure that each comb will be durable and strong. When this process is complete, the wedges are bound tightly into bundles and stored to prevent warping before they are ready to be sawed into teeth.

Takeuchi-san uses old-fashioned Japanese hand-planes, saws, and files. One item you might expect to find in his toolbox is a ruler for measuring and marking the location of each tiny tooth. He doesn't have one; a steady hand and practiced eye are the only instruments he uses. This process requires concentration. Takeuchi-san used to work in his shop on busy Shijo Street, but now does all the exacting parts of the process at his home in a quiet suburb east of Kyoto. His business dates to his great-grandfather's era in 1868. He opened the present shop on Shijo in 1930 at a time when the neighborhood still kept a slower pace. The fine finishing process is what makes the boxwood combs worth the extra yen they cost. Each tooth is polished with sharkskin then with dried *tokusa* (a hollow reed with a coarse inner texture), and finally buffed to a golden sheen with a soft deerskin cloth. No one can convince Takeuchi-san that sandpaper and an electric

buffer produce a finer finish than techniques like these that have been used in Japan since the tenth century.

The simplest boxwood combs Takeuchi-san makes bear only his family crest engraved on the side, but there are several more decorative styles carved with plum blossom, bamboo, and other traditional designs. Takeuchi-san and his son also make plain and lacquered *kanzashi*, the ornamental hairpins worn with formal kimono. Especially beautiful are the long, slender hair ornaments carved in the shape of a gingko leaf, in boxwood or cherry. In the old

KAGOSHIN
bamboo

The proudest day of Shintaro Morita's life was the day in 1920 when he climbed into the Imperial roadster that would carry him to the Old Palace to receive a special award from the emperor for his role in the introduction of bamboo ware to the West. Since 1862, he had made some of the finest bamboo basketry in Japan and had drawn the attention of buyers in the West to an art form previously overlooked abroad. His old bamboo shop still clings to the same spot on the north side of Sanjo-dori where it first opened for business, though it is engulfed today in modern buildings, mid-town traffic, and the noise of the Keihan train as it rumbles past on its way to Lake Biwa.

During the Edo period, Sanjo-dori was the last stretch of the Old Tokaido Highway, which connected Kyoto with Edo (now Tokyo), 488 kilometers to the east. A hundred years ago, there were many bamboo shops here beside the highway, as it was a direct route for transporting bamboo from the lush forests of Shiga. The bamboo supply in Shiga has been depleted over the years and only a few of the old bamboo shops in this area remain. Now Morita-san must go to Muko-machi in the southwest of Kyoto, where a good, though dwindling, supply of bamboo is still available. With an island climate just right for growing bamboo, the Japanese have explored every possible use for the flexible material, from water pipes to umbrella ribbings. One old account lists over fourteen hundred uses in all. Times have changed, however, and aluminum and plastics now perform most of the everyday jobs bamboo once handled so gracefully. Today Kagoshin produces fine bamboo baskets primarily for tea-ceremony utensils and flower arrangement, as well as a variety of ornamental *sode-gake* garden-fence "sleeves."

One of the most interesting types of bamboo used in basket weaving is called *susu-dake*, old bamboo recycled from the soot-darkened ceilings of Japanese farmhouses. The rich, natural patina this *susu-dake* acquires is highly prized when woven into fine basketry, and the limited supply makes it quite expensive. It can be distinguished from artificially stained bamboo by the alternating dark and light areas on each piece, the result of the bamboo having

days, every bride received an elaborate set of boxwood combs as a necessary part of her trousseau. They were used to dress the exotic hairstyles called *marumage* worn by married women up until World War II. Today only geisha and kabuki actors require comb sets like these, but a glass case at the back of Jusan-ya holds a large display.

Aside from the appreciation he has for the traditional methods of making combs for everyday use, there is another reason why Takeuchi-san maintains a craft that most people consider outdated. It has been his family's responsibility for generations to make the set of ninety-one combs that is offered in a special ceremony every twenty years to the goddess Amaterasu at Ise Shrine, the center of Shinto in Japan. At this time, the main buildings at Ise Shrine and all the treasures contained therein are destroyed. Fortunately, there are twenty years between the rites, because that is how long it takes to prepare the wood to make the exquisite set. How does it feel to devote two decades to the making of a perfect set of combs that you know are destined for destruction? "It's wonderful," says Takeuchi-san, "the greatest honor of my life."

been lashed to the roof beams with hemp cord.

Basketry is not the simple craft it may appear to be. Freshly cut bamboo must be dried for two years before it can be worked, as witnessed by ever-present stacks of stalks (some several meters long) drying out in front of Kagoshin. Before use, each individual stalk must be evaluated for shape and quality. For basket weaving, each stalk must be split and shaved to the appropriate width and thickness to suit the particular design. No two stalks of bamboo are identical, and the most difficult part of bamboo craftsmanship, according to Morita-san, is that each piece has an irrepressible character of its own and must be dealt with individually.

When asked if he hadn't considered tearing down his hundred-year-old shop and rebuilding in a way that would spare him from the street noise and exhaust, he replied, "How could I tear this place down? My customers like the old atmosphere. They would certainly complain—and besides, that room upstairs is where my grandfather made a bamboo chair for the emperor on his coronation day! How could I destroy a room like that?"

MIYAWAKI BAISEN-AN
fans

宮脇売扇庵

Art has surely sounded its lowest depths when it comes to portraying a lager-beer bottle on one side of a fan, and to providing a railway time-table on the other.

B. H. Chamberlain (1904)

Since the turn of the century, Westerners have been upbraiding the Japanese for busying themselves with modernization while age-old traditions die at their feet. Basil Hall Chamberlain missed out on the real tragedy: television commercials do all the advertising these days, and fans are no longer needed at all.

Once commonplace in Kyoto, the old round *uchiwa* fans now appear mainly during annual festivals or as wall decorations for those who delight in nostalgia.

Fortunately for Kyoto, Miyawaki Baisen-an has been making beautiful fans since 1823 and still believes in them today. Fans are important in Kyoto, not only as a means of fighting off the summer heat, but as eloquent accessories no Kyoto lady should be without. Earrings, pendants, bracelets, and rings are not suitable accessories for the simple lines of the kimono. Apart from hair ornaments and a single brooch on the cord that binds the *obi* sash, a Japanese woman's most eloquent accessory has always been a hand-painted, delicately scented folding fan.

Although many of the arts associated with Japan originated in China, the *sensu*, or folding fan, is said to have been an invention of the Japanese. (They even say the Japanese accused their continental neighbors of pirating technological secrets when the Chinese adopted the *sensu* in the fourteenth century.) Japanese legend attributes the invention of the first folding fan to a beautiful young woman who entered a nunnery after the death of her warrior husband. When the abbot of the temple fell sick, she made a fan of folded paper to ease his fever.

A folding-cypress fan *(hi-ogi)* dated 877, found inside a statue of Kannon at Toji temple, is considered to be the oldest in the world. There are many references to fans belonging to members of the Imperial Court during the Heian period, and by the end of the period even the common people

were using them. Painted wooden fans, scented sandalwood fans, lacquered fans with decorations in gold and silver, dyed silk fans, and paper fans all belong to one of Kyoto's oldest traditional crafts.

Miyawaki Baisen-an has fans of every description, each with its own special name: *Rikyu-ogi*, tea-ceremony fans named after the famous sixteenth-century tea master Sen no Rikyu; *hi-ogi*, or court fans; *mai-ogi*, fans used in traditional dance; *uchiwa*, the stiff, flat fan that originated in China; *chukei*, used in Noh theater; and ordinary *sensu* carried by both men and women to add an air of elegance (and a cooling breeze) to a formal kimono ensemble.

Every famous Japanese painter has decorated at least one fan in his time, making this an example of a Japanese craft that overlaps with the world of fine art. The ceiling of Miyawaki Baisen-an is covered with forty-eight paintings by master artists commissioned by the Miyawaki family in 1903, including an orchid-

and-rock fan painting by Tomioka Tessai and a tiger fan by Seiho Takeuchi.

The building that houses the fan shop is a treasure among the old shops of Kyoto. The Miyawakis have maintained this hundred-year-old structure, adding modern lighting and the comfort of air-conditioning without marring its old elegance. Each day when the shop opens for business the *batari shogi* bench in front folds down to give customers a place to rest; it folds back up each evening to become a part of the storm shutters that protect the building against the elements. The deep eaves and the black *noren* curtains that bear the shop's name hide the gilded fans from the damaging rays of the sun.

Miyawaki Baisen-an gives hope to those who, like Chamberlain, would like to see the best elements of the past survive. There is not a lager-beer advertisement or a train timetable in the place.

MORITA WAGAMI
handmade paper

Writing is easy; all you do is sit staring at a blank sheet of paper until the drops of blood form on your forehead.
Gene Fowler

Blank sheets of paper have been frightening artists and writers for a very long time. The Chinese were the first to suffer the silent taunting of the empty page: they've been writing poetry on paper longer than the West has been numbering the years.

The Japanese had paper in production for over five hundred years before the Moors opened the first paper mill in Spain in the twelfth century. By the end of the Edo period in 1868, the Japanese had figured out a way to use it for everything: lanterns, doors, windows, fans, candy wrappers, love letters, government orders, umbrellas, and even raincoats. The Tokugawa shoguns wrote their daily edicts on it, and it was no doubt a simple paper plot that finally brought the shogunate down. Paper has been absorbing mankind's mistakes and schemes, ideas and feelings, images and dreams for centuries, and nowhere more beautifully than in Japan.

Morita Wagami has a cure for nervous writers and artists everywhere—paper so peerless it's actually encouraging. It deals exclusively in handmade Japanese paper (*washi*), with a catalog of over eight hundred kinds from papermaking villages all over Japan.

Particular regions in Japan have become famous for the production of special kinds of paper. Echizen to the northeast of Kyoto is known for the finest white *hosho*, used as official stationery by the Imperial Court during the Edo period. Kurodani, a small village within three hours of Kyoto to the northwest, produces a rustic paper with a quality Morita-san calls "*majime-sa*"—honesty or earnestness.

Morita Wagami has *washi* for formal Japanese *shodo* calligraphy, contemporary Nihonga painting, and *hanga* printmaking.

Though many calligraphers use the less expensive Chinese papers for practice (sometimes five hundred tries are needed to produce a single character suitable for mounting), Morita-san stresses that Japan produces the very best and most durable

handmade paper in the world today, essential for professional artists who cannot afford to risk using paper that may yellow or crumble.

In the now modern gift shop beside the old paper warehouse a variety of paper products are also sold—from stationery, postcards, and notebooks to round *uchiwa* fans and miniature folding screens (*byobu*). It has the largest selection of decorated *chiyogami* paper in Kyoto. *Chiyogami*, or "long life" paper, was originally used by the aristocracy to wrap congratulatory gifts.

During the eighteenth and nineteenth centuries, *chiyogami* was considered a precious souvenir for people returning to their homes in the countryside from a trip to Kyoto or Edo (now Tokyo); it is interesting to compare *Kyo-chiyogami* (Kyoto style), with its reserved patterns and subdued colors, with the flamboyant designs and colors of *Edo-chiyogami*. The contrast between the restrained tastes of the people of the ancient capital and the riotous preferences of the townsfolk of Edo is apparent in matters as simple as package wrapping.

There are five basic techniques used in the making of decorative paper: *suki-zome*, a process in which the paper is made from pre-dyed materials; *shitashi-zome* or *wa-zome*, in which the paper is dyed with natural colors; *hake-zome*, or stencil-dyed paper; and *hanga*, which utilizes the woodblock printing technique.

The stencils for paper dyeing cost less than those for kimono dyeing, though they are cut by the same craftsmen out of the same materials. Considering the lower price the finished product will bring the paper dyer, the cost of the stencils is set proportionately lower. Relationships among Kyoto craftsmen and merchants are built on considerations such as these.

NAITO
brooms and brushes

Anna otoko wa hoki de haku hodo aru. (That kind of man is as plentiful as broom sweepings; i.e., Men like him are a dime a dozen.)

A good broom—just like a good man—is getting harder and harder to find these days, and they usually cost a good deal more than a dime a dozen. But one shop in Kyoto still has the real thing. Across the Sanjo Bridge from Keihan Train Station, the Naito family has been dealing in handmade brooms and brushes for over 120 years.

Naito was built in 1869 and is typical of Kyoto merchant shops dealing in practical items for everyday use—the kind in most danger of vanishing. Their wares are displayed hanging from the walls and rafters, with a raised shop floor in one corner at the back where the proprietress sits chatting with customers over a cup of tea, helping them choose "the right tool for the right job."

Unlike many similar shopkeepers whose busi-nesses now face a crowded modern thoroughfare, Sachiko Naito has never found it necessary to enclose her shop in metal-frame sliding glass doors. It remains as it always has been—open to the street—a part of the bustling activity of Sanjo-dori just outside. Mrs. Naito insists that her old shop will hold its own since her son, Hisayuki, has agreed to carry it on after her.

She remembers a time when the shop sold dozens of brooms a day. When her husband Rikimatsu Naito, a fifth-generation broom maker, passed away fifteen years ago, no one was left to carry on the family trade, a difficult and time-consuming business that requires strong muscles and leaves hands calloused. Now the shop sells brooms made by his former apprentices and friends, who are among the last remaining traditional broom makers in Kyoto. According to Mrs. Naito, when these men pass on, their trade will die with them.

Mrs. Naito has brooms and brushes in a variety of sizes and materials to fit the job as well as the

sweeper. There is a broom or brush for everything: one for cleaning your *hanko* (seal), another for ashtrays, others for the corners of desk drawers, toilet bowls, the collars of shirts, rusty iron kettles, the wooden frames of *shoji* windows, or simply for brushing the crumbs off your kitchen table. There is also an assortment of wonderful body brushes made of *shuro* or horsehair, to which many elderly residents of Kyoto attribute their good health.

Soft enough to sweep tatami mats, *shuro-boki* brooms are made of palm fibers brought to Kyoto from the outlying prefectures where they are grown. The soft bristles of the *shuro-boki* are designed especially for sweeping tatami, and though they are more expensive than mass-produced brooms, they last a good twenty years.

The other kind of broom featured at Naito is the *kibi-boki* (millet-stalk broom). These are the stiff green or yellow brooms for sweeping hardwood floors and rugs. Resembling their Western counterparts, the *kibi-boki* last only three to five years and are less expensive than *shuro-boki*; but they are hand-tied with colorfully dyed cord, making them quite unexpectedly an art form all their own.

The largest broom in the shop hangs in a dark corner at the back and is Naito-san's most valued keepsake from days gone by. Made by her great-grandfather a hundred years ago, it has taken on a deep brown patina. Although it has been grasped by a thousand hands and swept as many floors, it still looks like new. The bristles of a handmade *shuro-boki* never fall out; they just gradually grow shorter.

The *shuro-boki*, however, are on the endangered species list in the world of Kyoto crafts. Passing the old broom shop amid the dense traffic on Sanjo-dori it is a comfort to glance in and find Mrs. Naito, engrossed in the morning paper and firmly ensconced as usual amidst her simply beautiful brooms.

NAKANISHI TOKU SHOTEN

中西徳商店

antique dolls

A half smile, the faultless restraint, the delicate features, the irreproachable whiteness: like a Noh mask, the face of a Japanese doll silently reveals the soul of an ancient, ambiguous land. They are windows onto the past, and the image they pose is a half-forgotten ideal of beauty. They demonstrate in three dimensions how people lived, what they wore, what was important to them, what they felt and did not say. The Japanese doll recounts centuries of history without the complication or inadequacy of language.

In Japanese, *ningyo*, the word that describes these figures, has a thousand-year-old history with its roots in the spirit world. Records from the Heian period show that figures called *hitogata* (another reading of the same characters) were used to draw evil spirits and illness away from afflicted human beings. Throwing the contaminated figure into a nearby stream was believed to rid the person of his or her misfortune. Paper figures used for the same purpose can still be found at shrines in Japan today. Another kind of *ningyo* was placed near the head of a newborn baby to act as a surrogate, absorbing misdirected mayhem and giving the new arrival a starting chance. These figures were enshrined in a place of honor and offerings were made to them, particularly on March 3 each year, the day of an ancient purification ceremony that is known today as Hina Matsuri, the Doll Festival.

Over the centuries the figures became more and more elaborate and by the mid-Edo period the festival was one of the major celebrations of the year. *Hina ningyo* were displayed in pairs, dressed as a nobleman and his lady, attended by servants and surrounded by an assortment of miniature household furnishings—if your household happened to be imperial, that is. Tiny flowering trees adorned the shelves as symbols of the season and of the Imperial Court.

The delicate domestic festival became a special day of celebration for girls—a day on which they learned what it meant to be a woman in Japan. The qualities *hina ningyo* portrayed were refinement and elegance, contentment and restraint: exactly what Japanese society had in mind for its future wives and mothers. During the Meiji period, scholars admon-

ished parents to teach their daughters the virtues of proper womanhood through the careful handling of *hina ningyo*. These dolls were never "played with" in a Western sense. Instead, once a year they were carefully unwrapped and displayed for neighbors and relatives to admire, during a visit that also included sipping *amazake*, the sweet, hot "ladies' drink," and sampling sweetcakes appropriate to the season.

Along with the *hina ningyo*, another type of doll that bears historical and cultural significance is the *musha ningyo*, or samurai doll, displayed on May 5th in an equally important festival day that is known today as Kodomo no Hi, or Children's Day, though it originated in a day specifically for boys and still carries the male connotations it did in the days of the samurai. With these armor-clad warrior

dolls, little boys were taught the manly virtues of loyalty and courage.

Kyoto is the place where the finest of Japanese dolls originated, and Nakanishi's Fine Arts on Furumonzen Street specializes in antique Kyoto dolls (*Kyo-ningyo*) of all kinds. It is twenty years since Mr. Nakanishi decided to turn his long-time hobby of collecting antique dolls into a full-time business. Today his shop on Furumonzen Street is one of the only shops in Kyoto that deals exclusively in antique Japanese dolls, and collectors of fine dolls come there from all over the world. In his spare time he carves Buddhist statues from wood, a hobby he took up a few years ago "to keep my mind alert." He feels that the wooden Buddhas he carves are a natural outgrowth of his interest in antique dolls—after all, the Buddha, too, had a human form.

SAIUNDO

Japanese-painting supplies

Saiundo, the "Painted Cloud Shop," was named by Tomioka Tessai, one of the great masters of Japanese literati-style painting and one of Saiun-do's best turn-of-the-century customers.

In 1863, Tsukio Fujimoto, himself an accomplished Kyoto painter, succumbed to the urgings of his painter friends and opened a shop selling the special colors he had formulated for use in his own work. Preparing them in separate porcelain dishes, Fujimoto called them *gansai* (face colors), for the subtle, transparent quality that his formulas produced. Unlike the cumbersome mineral colors (*iwa-enogu*), which must be ground with a mortar and pestle and mixed with a special medium (*nikawa*, or hide glue) before they can be applied, Fujimoto's colors were obtained from plant pigments and were water soluble, making them ideal for the delicate washes applied to *suiboku-ga*, or ink paintings.

Saiundo is run today by Fujimoto's great-grandson and carries all the supplies necessary for Japanese painting—brushes (over a hundred kinds), inks, paints, water containers, brush holders, undercloths, even handmade paper. They have brushes for every imaginable purpose, from a six-inch-wide *hake* flat brush for temple-door–sized washes, to an impossibly fine *kegaki* brush for painting the hairs on a brow. There are even special *ten-tsuki* brushes for painting dots or tears. One type of brush thought to be unique to Japan is the *renpitsu*, which is actually five separate brushes bound together with a single handle. The *renpitsu* is used for large sweeps of color where a gradation of shades is desired with one stroke. Unlike the broad, flat *hake* brush, the combination of individually pointed brushes in the *renpitsu* is designed to produce a clean, sharp edge of deep color that fades to a lighter overall wash with one stroke.

Saiundo's guest book lists world-famous painters and designers from New York, Paris, and Tokyo—artists who have come to appreciate the beauty of a handmade badger-hair (*tanuki-ke*) brush for fine detail work, or a sheep-hair (*hitsuji-ke*) brush for applying color washes.

Aside from specialized supplies for professional painters, Fujimoto-san can also provide the

novice with everything needed to begin painting in the *suiboku-ga* or *sumi-e* style. *Sumi-e* is the term most commonly known in the West, but both refer to monochrome ink painting and include those efforts that sometimes have a splash of color.

Among the tools and supplies required are an all-purpose *suketate* brush, capable of producing a fine line as well as a sweeping wash; a traditional *shitajiki* felt cloth to place under paper; *sumi* ink sticks ranging in tones from blue to brown; a *suzuri* ink-grinding stone; a square *hissen* water vessel for rinsing brushes; a set of small white porcelain bowls for mixing colors; a package of off-white *gassen-shi* paper for practicing and a twelve- to sixteen-color set of *gansai* paints that provides the full range of traditional Japanese colors using the original secret formulas developed by Fujimoto-san's great-grandfather over a hundred years ago. But why stop there? The lover of fine, handmade things may well find the beautiful cast-metal paperweights, handmade bamboo brush

cases, painted porcelain water containers, and hand-braided silk scroll tassels irresistible.

Saiundo's one-room shop was built in the late Edo period and has the intimate atmosphere of the traditional Kyoto shop dealing in very specialized products for a limited clientele. Seated on tatami behind a low wooden desk, Mr. Fujimoto weighs small packets of powdered mineral colors (*iwa-enogu*) and chunks of dissolving (*suihi*) colors to fill the stack of orders from the many artists of the contemporary Nihonga Japanese painting school, who prefer the thick crystalline texture that the mineral paints provide.

Fujimoto-san is knowledgeable and friendly, and though he says that he barely manages in English, the number of world-famous foreign artists in his guest book attests to his ability to communicate. It gives him as much pleasure, he says, to advise an earnest beginner as to serve Japan's greatest master.

NISHIHARU
woodblock prints

Ukiyo-e are images from the "floating world," the mundane and mortal world that slips from our hands and leaves us with only the memory of squandered fortunes and ill-spent youth. Beautiful winsome women, the light of neglected oil lamps flickering out at daybreak, the painted flowers of a priceless silk kimono lying in disarray on the floor where it was flung in a moment of careless passion—the excesses of a world that no longer exists live on in *ukiyo-e*, the woodblock prints that depict life in the entertainment quarters of Edo-period Japan.

Nishiharu is the oldest shop in Kyoto dealing exclusively in antique woodblock prints. It has stood for sixty-five years on the corner of Teramachi and Sanjo, once the hub of downtown activity, silently watching the transformation that has left it and one or two of its old neighbors amid a circus of new souvenir shops and glittering *pachinko* parlors.

The shopkeeper, Mr. Tohru Sekigawa, believes in doing business in the old style. No random piles of prints stacked here and there in disarray, cluttering glass showcases—just one small tatami-mat room with a single scroll hanging in the alcove, and a cup of tea and courtesy waiting for every customer. His carefully selected collection of antique *ukiyo-e* prints is tucked neatly away in lacquered boxes and old cabinet drawers waiting to be unveiled, one by one, at the customer's request.

Although this style of business is intended for the buyer who knows what to ask for, Mr. Sekigawa is happy to bring out dozens of prints for the novice who shows a real interest in this fascinating art form. You can ask to see prints by specific artists: Hiroshige, Utamaro, Kuniyoshi, Hokusai, Sharaku, and others. Or you may ask to see those of a particular genre: *bijin-ga*, portraits of beautiful women; *yakusha-e*, portraits of kabuki actors; *fukei-ga*, prints depicting the scenery; *fuzoku-ga*, or pictures of the way of life in the city.

Mr. Sekigawa advises that you ask to see more than one impression of the print you choose, as other editions were sometimes made from the original woodblocks at a later date. It is generally true that the first impression is the best, not only because the

blocks themselves were new, but because the artist was there to supervise the choice of colors. His prints are not offered at bargain prices; those available elsewhere for less, he says, tend to be in poor condition or are merely copies of an original. He sells no print that cannot be identified as to age and artist, and every print is tagged with this basic information in Japanese and English, as many of his regular buyers are collectors from abroad. He guarantees every piece he sells to be authentic.

His advice on the care and display of *ukiyo-e* is simply to keep them out of direct sunlight because ultraviolet rays cause color changes, particularly in the green hues. Hang your print for no more than three months out of the year, but don't store it too long without airing it for a few days in a dry place. Dry climates are better than wet for the preservation of woodblock

A sizzling summer afternoon in the heart of the city and Tomii-san draws an ice-cold bucket of water from his well for his foreign interviewer to refresh her face and hands. He props an electric fan on top of a giant wooden washtub, sits me down in front of it, and asks me how I like the weather and what I'd like to know.

"Tell me about the man in the picture," I say, pointing to the emaciated figure in white robes in the photo on the wall in back.

"Oh, that's Sakae-san. He's a holy man. He's my friend," Tomii-san replies. Sakae-san had just completed a strenuous Buddhist austerity, called *sen-nichi kaiho gyo*, in which he walked a circuit of twenty-five miles a night around Mt. Hiei north of Kyoto—a thousand nights over a period of seven years. At the end of his ordeal he ate nothing for nine days; it clears the mind. During the final stage of fasting and prayer, severely weakened by his long ordeal, Sakae-san carried a pair of Taruden's wooden buckets—full of water—suspended from both ends of a pole over his shoulder from a well to a sacred site, where a purification ritual was then performed. One of Tomii-san's greatest sources of pride is having made the buckets that Sakae-san carried.

Sakae-san may be a saint, but his friend Tomii-san is very down-to-earth. Tomii insists, however, that his family has always had a connection with the world of spirits. The family well stood inside the precincts of an old shrine at one time and provided water for the purification of its worshippers. Over 120 years ago, Tomii-san's great-grandfather found an old book on the grounds of the shrine. It was a bucket maker's pattern book. With an omen from heaven that clear, he began making buckets.

A middle-aged neighbor appeared as we sat talking. She announced that her eighty-year-old mother could no longer bear life without a wooden washtub. Tomii-san was out of washtubs that day and apologized. Spying the used tub on top of which the fan was perched, she said, "Well, how about that one?" Perhaps understanding how adamant an eighty-year-old lady can be, Tomii-san extricated the large tub, doused it with well water, scrubbed it down with a bristle brush, and tied it to the back of

prints, which are highly sensitive to humidity. *Ukiyo-e* are sought after not only by art collectors, but by rodents and insects, who devour them with unparalleled zeal. It is best to store them with ordinary mothballs in a pest-free location.

Beyond making structural repairs when necessary, Mr. Sekigawa has no plans to modernize his shop in the future. He tried carpeting the tatami and moving in a desk after the previous owner passed away some years ago. "In the end," he says, sliding out an elegant lacquered tray with a fresh cup of tea, "I decided tatami was best for spreading out my prints and chatting with customers. Besides, nothing pleases me more than talking with a middle-aged lady on a trip to Kyoto from the countryside who stops in to tell me how happy she is to find my shop just as she remembers it from a school excursion to Kyoto thirty years ago."

her bicycle. "I know what you mean," he said. "The old folks just don't believe that these newfangled washing machines can get a collar clean enough." As his customer pedaled off with a satisfied grin, he turned to me with scrub brush in hand and said, "I haven't been sick one day in forty years. It's because I use one of these old scrub brushes on my back!"

Both Tomii-san and his buckets are sturdy. His cedar bath buckets last thirty to forty years with daily use, if properly dried in the sun whenever possible.

The lidded casks (*taru*) for storage, and carrying buckets (*oke*), are made from designs and techniques described by his great-grandfather in an old note-book, one of his prized possessions. Special handmade curved planes called *kanna* form the exact angle of each curved stave, depending on the diameter of the particular bucket to be made. Like most traditional woodworkers in Japan, Tomii-san makes all his tools himself. The staves are held together by tiny bamboo dowels joining every seam, the perfect workmanship

YAMATO MINGEI-TEN
folk art

We must bring back...those days when all things required in ordinary daily life were beautiful.
Soetsu Yanagi, *The Unknown Craftsman*

With these thoughts, one of the leaders of the Mingei (Folk Art) Movement noted the loss of appreciation for naturally made, simple objects—brooms, baskets, bowls, buckets, and ladles—that were once commonplace in Japan. Yanagi, a philosopher and critic, Kanjiro Kawai, Shoji Hamada, Bernard Leach, and a handful of others in the 1920s attempted to save what was left of Japan's unpretentious country craftsmen by calling attention to their plight in a rapidly industrializing society infatuated with the West.

The founders of the Mingei Movement were not interested in the individual artist-craftsmen who produced a limited number of precious objects more decorative than functional in purpose. These "art pieces" were affected and self-conscious, they believed, lacking the rustic beauty of unsigned works produced in rural villages across the country.

The members of the movement set about collecting the everyday objects they so much admired, making trips as far as Korea and Okinawa to remote areas as yet unaffected by modernization. The objects they gathered are now kept in the Tokyo Folkcraft Museum in Komaba, which Yanagi and his friends founded in 1936. They hoped to preserve a wide selection of fine folk crafts for future craftsmen to use as inspiration even after the tiny villages from which the objects came had joined the ranks of concrete and stucco.

But the craftsmen themselves were in need of help that no museum could offer. As the population turned its back on folk crafts as crude and old-fashioned, the livelihood of the country craftsmen declined until many were forced to seek other employment, to use synthetic materials and mass-production techniques, or to starve.

Shortly after World War II, a man named Yaei Hayashi, at the suggestion of friends in the Mingei Movement, came to the aid of Japan's folk craftsmen by opening a shop in the middle of Kyoto that sold nothing but folk crafts from all over Japan. Now run by his daughter Akiko, Yamato Mingei-ten on

creating a bucket that holds water even before the bamboo or copper ring is put around it.

Some of Taruden's buckets are used by Urasenke, the world-famous school of tea just across Horikawa Street to the east, in preparation for each New Year's ceremony. Bucket-shaped flower vases are also popular with local tea masters in search of objects that possess a sense of simplicity and unpretentious dignity. Taruden makes several different shapes and sizes of flower vases in cypress (*sawaragi*), all with the prized, natural, unvarnished finish.

Tomii-san, unfortunately, has no son and no apprentice to carry on his vanishing trade. But meeting him now and visiting his two-hundred-year-old shop, with the bright-red buckets out front his only "signboard," offers reassurance—if only temporarily—that you haven't arrived in Kyoto too late.

Kawaramachi-dori still sells the finest in folk crafts gathered from villages from Hokkaido to Okinawa.

The highly refined crafts produced in the city of Kyoto itself have never been considered "folk," but many of the villages in the surrounding area, such as Kurodani, where paper is made, rank among the finest crafts villages in Japan.

The selection at Yamato is always changing, and every month different crafts from different areas are featured along with the impressive stock of ceramics, glassware, lacquer ware, basketry, and textiles. Hand-made Japanese paper (*te-suki washi*) from Echizen or Kurodani, lacquered bowls from Wajima, baskets from Miyajima, blown glass from Okinawa, Nanbu teakettles from Iwate—all are made with traditional techniques and materials and tagged with the name of the area from which they came. In keeping with Yanagi's views that *mingei* objects should also be affordable, the prices at Yamato Mingei-ten are reasonable, especially considering the value of hand-made objects in modern times.

The main shop faces Kawaramachi-dori and sells a wide variety of smaller items; the branch shop on the alley south of Maruzen has larger objects— furniture from Tottori and hand-hewn stone basins and lanterns from the Kita-Shirakawa district in northeastern Kyoto. The branch shop also holds exhibitions that feature works by different craftsmen or from different crafts villages each month, and occasionally includes exhibitions of folk crafts from around the world.

SHOYEIDO

incense

L ife goes up in smoke—fleeting, gone before
you know it; it rises, fades, disappears. In
Buddhism, *o-ko*, or incense, is a reminder
of that evanescent quality of life. For those practicing
Zen meditation, it is a way to mark the passage of
time without the necessity of dividing it into minutes
and seconds. The dying stick of incense defines an
interval of silence, the composure of meditation; the
moments are, as the saying goes, "so quiet you can
hear the powdered ash of incense fall." Brought
from China to Japan in the sixth century, *o-ko* is
still an important part of Buddhist ritual today.

Appealing as it does to the senses, incense also
possesses age-old associations with the pursuit of
pleasure. The wide range of scents developed over
the centuries throughout the world appeal to the
vulnerable human psyche with everything from the
excitement of an aphrodisiac to the quieting effects
of a midnight snowfall.

Like Japanese cuisine, *o-ko* is always a subtle

and complex experience. Over the centuries, the
enjoyment of incense in Japan has evolved into a
refined and subtle art. Long before the tea ceremony,
the nobles of the Imperial Court in Kyoto amused
themselves with a game called *ko-awase*, a guessing
game in which participants tried to name different
scents as they were lit, one by one, by their host.

The aromatic woods and spices combined to
create these fragrances were expensive and difficult
to obtain in the days of Prince Genji. Rare ingredients
were imported from all over Asia and the South
Seas, including Java, Sumatra, and India, as none of
the raw materials were indigenous to Japan. It was
not until much later, in the Muromachi period, that
the game became formalized into a ritual called
kodo (the Way of Incense) that reached its peak of
popularity in the Edo period.

Shoyeido has made fine incense for almost
three hundred years. Founded in 1705, it is one of
the oldest and most respected incense makers in

Japan, dealing in the finest incense available in the country. The present eleventh-generation head of the company is Shigetaro Hata. It was his great-grandfather who first introduced *ko* to the West when he took samples of cone incense, one of his own inventions, to the World Exposition in Chicago in 1894. Shigetaro's son, Masataka Hata, the director of Shoyeido, actively shares his knowledge of incense with the West by performing *kodo*, at which he is a master, to appreciative audiences around the world.

Incense used for personal enjoyment today is derived from aromatic woods, from herbs and spices and from flowers. Perhaps the most intriguing of these are the aromatic woods. Sandalwood (*byakudan*), aloeswood (*jinko*), and resinated aloeswood (*kyara*) are the three main kinds. Sold in chips or granules, some are taken from root sections of the trees, some from green wood, and some from pieces found buried for a thousand years. The older the piece, the more earthy, subtle, and expensive the fragrance.

Unlike *senko* (the stick form of incense), *wari-byakudan* or *wari-jinko* (the wood-chip varieties) must be burned in small charcoal incense burners. Fine blends of incense in stick form are available, though many of them are more pungent and insistent than the natural woods, which are a bit more troublesome to burn. A lighted piece of charcoal (*sumi*) is placed in the center of a mound of ash in a ceramic or metal *koro* burner. Over this, a small square of transparent mica is set to shield the incense from the direct heat, then the mica is covered with ash, leaving just a small opening in which to place the incense. This method allows a long, slow burning and affords the most delicate aroma.

The language of fine fragrance defies words. The verb *kagu*, to smell, is not used in referring to the world of incense. The Japanese prefer to use *kiku*, to hear—perhaps in an effort to describe an experience that appeals as much to a sixth sense as it does to the other five.

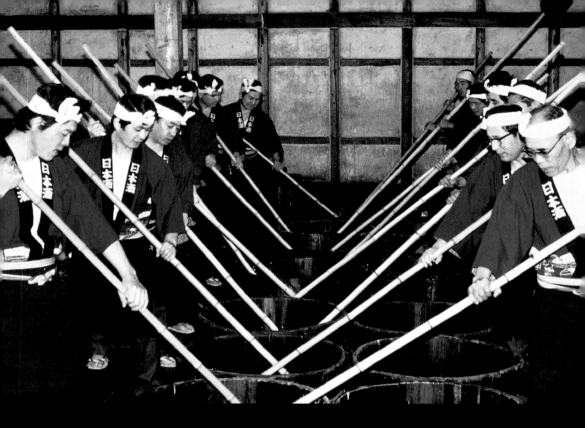

Fuka	*fu* (wheat gluten)
Gekkeikan	saké brewery
Ippodo	tea
Iriyama Tofu	tofu
Murakami-Jū	pickles
Narita	pickles
Shoyosei-Ken	Kyoto confectionery
Tsukimochiya Naomasa	Kyoto confectionery
Yubahan	*yuba* (soy milk "skins")

FUKA
wheat gluten

Only the people of Kyoto, perhaps, could take a food as simple as wheat gluten and turn it into the versatile *fu*. A local specialty served as a dainty sweet with tea or used as a decorative touch in Kyoto cuisine, *fu* was once a basic source of protein in the vegetarian diet of Buddhist monks in China. Now it comes in a variety of Kyoto disguises—a different color and shape for every season: pink cherry blossom *fu* in spring, bright-purple eggplant *fu* in summer, red and yellow maple-leaf *fu* in autumn, and festive New Year's ornament shapes for January 1. "Wheat gluten," though an accurate translation, hardly seems adequate in describing the popular delicacy known as *fu*.

Fuka, just west of the Old Imperial Palace grounds, has been making *fu* for 130 years. Shoji Kobori, the present owner, is the seventh-generation master of a shop once designated as an official purveyor to the Imperial Household.

There are two main types of *fu*: fresh (*nama-fu*) and dried (*yaki-fu*). Fuka makes only *nama-fu*, which is used frequently in the making of confectionery. *Sasamaki-fu* is one variety of *nama-fu* filled with sweet bean paste and beautifully wrapped in bamboo leaves to be served with green tea. Formed into shapes and colors evoking the seasons, *nama-fu* is used also in soups (without the sweet filling). *Rikyu-fu*, named after Sen no Rikyu, the tea master who popularized *fu* for use in the tea ceremony in the sixteenth century, is a variety of regular *fu* boiled in a spicy broth then deep-fried. It can be sliced and served cold as an appetizer with saké or beer.

During the Edo period *fu* became so popular that an entire street in downtown Kyoto still bears the name "Fuyacho-dori," after the many *fu* shops that once lined it. Today, only a few *fu* specialty shops remain in Kyoto.

The traditional process of making *fu* was both simple and back-breakingly hard work. A plain wheat dough was made of flour and water and kneaded for two long hours to bring out the gluten. Today, a modern blender is used. Next the dough is placed under water and kneaded again until it separates into its two basic elements, starch and gluten. The starch floats to the surface, and the gluten remains. It is

food, blending ingredients such as pumpkin and even bacon with the batter to the applause of many dyed-in-the-wool traditional *fu* connoisseurs.

Kobori-san is an easygoing man who is generally unimpressed by the fuss made over so-called *shinise*, the name given to revered old Kyoto shops. "Too many places rely on an established name and use the *Kyo-* (Kyoto) prefix on their products as if that alone ensured quality," he says. "My family has been making *fu* for generations, and our shop has become famous for it, but good *fu* is made all over Japan nowadays. Relying on '*Kyo*-this' and '*Kyo*-that' doesn't make it the best. I just try to make the finest product I can."

月桂冠

GEKKEIKAN
saké brewery

There is a song that the saké makers of Fushimi sang as they toiled through the night, stirring fermenting rice with long-handled wooden paddles to prepare the *moto*, or yeast mash, for the marathon task of making saké, the traditional rice brew of Japan. It tells of a young man who has wanted all his life to be able to work in the great saké breweries of Fushimi. When his lucky break finally comes and he finds himself toiling throughout the cold winter night over steaming tubs of rice, he has second thoughts. He bemoans the icy mornings when he has to wash the rice and wishes he hadn't been quite so hasty in his choice of employment. In the end, he muses, his efforts will result in delicious Fushimi saké—but there is a touch of irony in his words that implies he'll never be the one to taste it.

Since the seventeenth century, the great saké breweries, or *kura*, of Fushimi have hired farmers

from Echizen and Tango in the north near the Japan Sea to come to Kyoto during their idle winter months to make what was once the saké of samurai.

The eldest, most experienced of the workers were known as *toji*, the master brewers. They brought with them the hard-earned knowledge of generations of saké makers who had spent one hundred days of constant, back-breaking work each year to make Fushimi one of the main centers of saké production in Japan. Although the major saké companies now have ultramodern factories, elaborately temperature-controlled to produce saké all the year round, many of the smaller makers still employ the *toji* each year from the same families that have

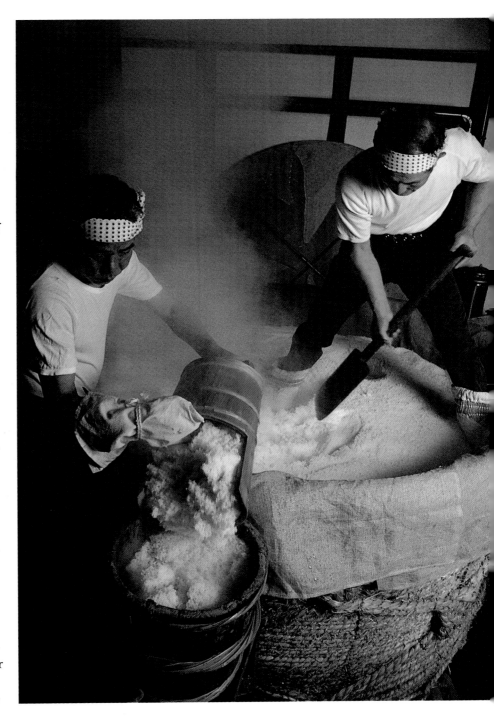

worked in their *kura* for centuries using the same ancient techniques.

Gekkeikan, the makers of the world's best-selling saké, haven't forgotten the debt they owe the generations of *toji* who have served the company faithfully for over three hundred years. Although the company now possesses the most advanced, best-equipped brewery in the country, Gekkeikan insists on maintaining the original tile-roofed *kura* in which *toji* have worked for centuries. Its five modern, computerized factories now work year-round producing 135,000 bottles of top-quality saké a day to be served in homes and restaurants around the world. But beside a willow-lined canal not far from the Keihan Train Station at Chushojima (fifteen minutes south of Kyoto), in a huge, tile-roofed *kura* of Gekkeikan, *toji* still produce a limited amount of *te-zukuri* (handmade) saké, just as their predecessors have since 1637.

When Rokurouemon Okura first opened his brewery in Fushimi 350 years ago, he was one of many competing for the favor of the Tokugawa shogunate in an area that was already one of the two biggest saké producers in the country (the other being Nada near Osaka). Brewers had been flocking to Fushimi ever since Toyotomi Hideyoshi, the great military leader, started building his magnificent castle there in 1594.

Fushimi is located at the convergence of three major rivers, the Yodo, the Kamo, and the Katsura, and was a convenient stop for boatmen and traders plying the waterways and highways between Kyoto and Osaka. Fushimi was a saké brewer's dream—it had river access to the best rice available from Himeji. It had the chilly winters necessary for conducting the world's most finicky brewing process and some of the best underground spring water available. It had a castle full of thirsty samurai, who were possibly seventeenth-century Japan's most avid saké fans.

In 1905, the Okura family named its saké Gekkeikan, "laurel wreath," a name intended to symbolize the Olympian heights to which the company aspired. In 1914, the company was designated a Purveyor to the Imperial Household; today, it is the largest saké producer in the world.

IPPODO

tea

It is Ippodo's fault that everything within two blocks of the shop on Teramachi-dori is permeated with the enticing aroma of freshly roasted tea leaves. In fact, Ippodo has been perfuming the neighborhood for almost 150 years with the finest green tea from Uji, the most famous tea-producing region in Japan.

Uji, just south of Kyoto, where the round, carefully trimmed hedgerows of tea plants color the hills a vivid green, has the ideal climate for growing tea. Here on the foggy banks of the Uji River, the misty air and rich soil yield the best tea in the country.

Ippodo was once designated by the Imperial Household Agency as a Purveyor to the Imperial Family, though such designations were officially discontinued after World War II.

Until the twentieth century, tea was a luxury in which only the upper classes could indulge. Said to have been brought back from China by the Buddhist monk Eisai in 1191, it gained a vogue among the samurai when Sen no Rikyu perfected the tea ceremony

some four centuries later. For five hundred years, it was drunk in its powdered form, called *matcha*. In the mid-eighteenth century the process for making *sencha*, the rolled-leaf type of green tea, was discovered. Then with the introduction of a tea-processing machine in the early 1900s, the common people were finally initiated into the formerly exclusive pleasures of sipping fine green tea.

There are several different types of tea (*o-cha*) available at Ippodo: *matcha*, the powdered tea of the tea ceremony; *gyokuro*, a sweet, fragrant tea made with only the finest leaves from the tips of the best plants; *sencha* (the type most often served to guests in Japan today), a leaf tea from the same plants as *gyokuro*, but with a sharper astringency; *bancha*, a coarser leaf tea, the most common roasted variety; *hojicha*, a lightly roasted blend of *bancha* and *sencha*; *mugicha*, roasted with barley; and *Uji-shimizu*, a powder used for making iced green tea. Within each type of tea there are many varieties and grades; over thirty varieties of *matcha* alone are available, with

indications given as to which tea is preferred by which tea master. Many of Watanabe-san's foreign customers prefer the aromatic *hojicha* or the delicate *gyokuro*. Watanabe-san says that fine tea should not be stored for more than two weeks, and he recommends buying only forty-gram containers of *matcha* at a time.

Each year in May, the tea leaves are hand-picked in Uji, and connoisseurs look forward to sampling the *shincha*, or "new tea." In the seventeenth and eighteenth centuries, the Tokugawa shogunate halted all other traffic along the Tokaido Highway while the convoy bearing the annual shipment of *shincha* from Uji made its way to Edo.

The interior of Ippodo, lined with old tea jars along the north wall, remains remarkably unchanged. The building was constructed after the Tenmei Fire in 1864, which destroyed a large part of the city. The original shop, called Omiya and established in 1715, was located across the street. But in 1846 a nobleman who purchased tea there exhorted the shopkeeper to carry on his fine trade with the words "Promise you'll never sell anything but fine tea." From that day on the shop took the name Ippodo, freely translatable as "the shop that sticks to one thing."

At the old wooden counter, attentive clerks wait to brew a sample cup of whichever tea the customer would like to try, then carefully measure out the requested amount. Ippodo's airtight tea canisters, with their turn-of-the-century green and orange labels, are a treasure in themselves. Store your tea, in its container, in a cool place. It tastes best when used within two weeks. A general rule for brewing is to remember that the hotter the water, the more tannin is released, and the more bitter it becomes. The finest teas (*gyokuro*, *sencha*) are steeped at lower temperatures for a slightly longer time than the common teas (*hojicha*, *bancha*, *mugicha*), which are prepared in a larger ceramic teapot called a *dobin*.

O-cha has all the eye-opening, mind-clearing effects of coffee, without the strain on the stomach. The fresh, astringent flavor and the aroma of a cup of the finest tea from Ippodo may convert even the most inveterate coffee drinker to the fold of tea.

IRIYAMA TOFU

入山豆腐

tofu

Mame de	Made of beans
Shikaku de	Squarely cut
Yawarakaku te	And soft

When the priest Ingen wrote this poem in 1661, he was not only praising the qualities of good tofu, he was also implying something about the human spirit. *Mame* means both beans and diligence; *shikaku* means square or honest; and *yawarakai* means soft or gentle—a desirable combination in both bean curds and people.

Tofu is as much a part of the diet in Japan as cheese is in the West. High in protein and low in calories, this soybean product was first made in China over two thousand years ago. Tofu can be fried, simmered, grilled, and even eaten fresh, dipped in soy sauce and covered with diced green onions. Tofu is a simple food that absorbs and enhances the flavor of soups and broths, adding vital protein to the traditional Buddhist vegetarian diet. The

most frequent dishes in which it can be found in modern-day Japan are miso soup, *yu-dofu* (a one-pot simmered dish), *oden* (a stewlike dish with tofu and other specialties simmered in broth), and *hiya-yakko* (cold fresh tofu, popular in summer).

Few shops in modern Kyoto persist in the traditional methods of making tofu, but at Iriyama Tofu (if you rise early enough in the morning) you can watch a ninth-generation tofu maker whose ancestors made tofu for the Imperial Court in the early nineteenth century. Today the shop specializes in "cotton" tofu (*momen-goshi*), a more coarsely textured variety than the "silk" tofu (*kinu-goshi*) that has become popular supermarket fare in recent years. Cotton tofu has the ring of farmhouses and home-cooking that makes most fancy chefs in the pursuit of Kyoto-style elegance tend to turn up their noses, according to the unaffected Mrs. Iriyama.

"We don't make pretty tofu here," she says, fanning the charcoal fire with one hand as she turns

the skewered tofu with the other. An occasional charcoal cinder on the surface of Iriyama's grilled tofu (*yaki-dofu*) just adds to the flavor. Unlike many of the tofu shops in Japan today, Iriyama Tofu uses no chemical additives to gel its tofu. Instead it prefers to use refined *nigari* sea brine as a coagulant for the subtle sweetness it imparts, even if it is less predictable, especially during the hot, muggy summers for which Kyoto is notorious.

Two large vats of soybeans simmer over the old wood-burning cookstoves inside the 120-year-old building, which is located on the same site where the Iriyamas' ancestors cooked soybeans in the late Edo period. The sagging stone floors, old well, and crumbling clay ovens comfort each other in modern times when most other tofu makers have turned to concrete and stainless steel.

Mrs. Iriyama complains that once a delivery truck barreling down the narrow back street took out the west wall of the shop, plowing into the back of the old clay ovens in the process. It would have been easier to replace them with new gas-burning

stoves, but the Iriyamas felt that the traditional stoves cooked a better-tasting batch of beans. Finding someone who still knew how to make an old cookstove was a task in itself, almost as difficult as it is to find a tofu shop like this one in an age when many Kyoto housewives buy tofu at the supermarket. But they did find a craftsman, and though the stove resembles a giant anthill with a chimney, the "new" ovens crackle and shoot off sparks through the early morning hours at Iriyama Tofu just as the old ones did.

Momen-goshi tofu, deep-fried plain tofu (*o-age*), and deep-fried tofu mixed with sesame or chopped vegetables (*hirosu*) are available at Iriyama Tofu year-round. The grilled tofu (*yaki-dofu*), made fresh daily from autumn through spring, may have a coarser texture than that sold in local supermarkets, but the aroma of fresh soybean curd and the old-fashioned homemade flavor are well worth the wait for neighbors who bring their own containers and stand in line, sharing the latest local gossip, while the Iriyamas grin and sweat and grill their delicious tofu.

MURAKAMI-JU
pickles

"Feed not autumn eggplant to your daughter-in-law."

Don't spoil your son's blushing bride with needless luxury.... A spiteful old saying which, unlike the eggplant itself, is hardly worth preserving, except perhaps as a reminder of what was wrong with "the good old days."

The best locally grown vegetables, picked at the height of the season, have always been considered a delightful extravagance, especially in the form of Murakami-ju's *tsukemono*, or pickles. Pickled eggplant is only one of over twenty varieties of *tsukemono* found at this 150-year-old shop. Parting the dark-brown shop curtain bearing the cross-and-circle crest, you enter a space with rough-hewn stone floors and two giant wooden pickle barrels brimming with the day's selection of fresh *tsukemono*. A set of small ceramic crocks on the counter contain samples—*senmai-zuke* (paper-thin slices of white radish seasoned with red pepper and lightly sweetened with kelp) in winter, *nanohana-zuke* (flowers from the rapeseed plant lightly pickled in rice vinegar) in spring, *narazuke* (a variety of vegetables salt-pickled and soaked in saké) in summer.

Tsukemono were a primary source of nutrition in less prosperous times, when a bowl of rice or barley and a few pickled vegetables made up the entire meal for most Kyoto townsfolk. Living in a city located far from the sea and surrounded on three sides by mountains, the citizens of Kyoto had to develop methods of preserving food in a humid, mold-provoking climate. Essentially, *Kyo-ryori*, the sophisticated local cuisine, developed out of an assortment of salted fish and pickled vegetables, elaborately presented in an endlessly imaginative repertoire.

In frugal Kyoto, for example, not only radishes, but radish leaves and stems too are pickled. All kinds of peculiar roots and mountain ferns, leafy greens, and even flowers are pickled. But the vegetables most commonly used everywhere in Japan are radishes (*daikon*), cucumbers (*kyuri*), eggplant (*nasu*), and Chinese, or Napa, cabbage (*hakusai*). The oldest type of *tsukemono* in Japan is said to be *Nara-zuke*, the strong-flavored variety that is pickled in saké.

There are records of this kind of pickle dating from the Nara period, hence the name.

The most often served pickle is called *takuan*—crisp, round, deep-yellow slices of *daikon* that accompany the simplest meals in any family-style Japanese restaurant. *Takuan* is said to be a good digestive, and the tale goes that no matter how much raw fish or how many bowls of white rice you eat, a few slices of *takuan* will pull you through. The radishes are first dried in the sun, then placed in a wooden barrel with rice bran and salt, and a large stone is placed on the lid for pressure.

The making of *tsukemono* used to be a chore every housewife took for granted, but *daikon* drying on rooftops are a sight only seen these days in the countryside. *Tsukemono* fall into two basic categories: *furu-zuke*, pickles fermented for a time in a rice-bran mash with salt, which can be kept longer than usual, and *asa-zuke*, vegetables pickled in dry rice bran and salt, which must be eaten within a few days. Plain salt-pickling (*shio-zuke*) and vinegar-pickling (*su-zuke*) are simpler methods, but the rice bran gives the pickles a subtle depth of flavor. Murakami-ju has not succumbed to using artificial colors to entice supermarket shoppers, who tend to be attracted to the most eye-catching fluorescent pink *tsukemono* and pay no attention to expiration dates on packages (forcing major food suppliers to load their products with preservatives).

Unlike Western pickles, good *tsukemono* retain the crisp, natural taste of the vegetable itself.

Apart from their regular customers, Murakami-ju draws visitors from all over Japan, who make a special stop on their sightseeing tours to buy a package of the famous Kyoto-style *tsukemono*. On a busy day you may have to wait to be served, but the thoughtful cup of tea provided, and the floral arrangement in a giant ceramic urn in the center of the room, help the time to pass painlessly. Toru Murakami, the proprietor, believes in old-fashioned Kyoto hospitality and service, and spends much of his time coaching his youngest clerks in the proper way to sell a Kyoto pickle—graciously, honestly, and with style.

NARITA

pickles

Kamigamo Shrine, said to have been founded by the Kamo clan in the early sixth century. It is located in a strategic position in the north of Kyoto beside the Kamogawa River. During the Heian period the court awarded the shrine priests many estates, to ensure strong permanent ties, and a line of head priests descended from the imperial family was established.

By the seventeenth century, the area around the shrine had come to be known as a *shake machi*, literally a "shrine family township," with 275 houses in the area belonging to the families of the shrine priests. Today the area has been declared a historic preservation district, and the walled *shake machi* houses lining it retain much of the rural atmosphere that Kamigamo Shrine has kept for centuries, as a visit to the nearby Nishimura House will confirm.

Michiyasu Narita's pickle shop itself originally belonged to one of the *shake* families. The Naritas have restored the impressive two-hundred-year-old structure to its former glory; the stone and clay outer walls, the sweeping tile roofs, and the white-washed walls of the main building are typical of the *shake* houses in this area. A stone path leads through the gateway across a graveled courtyard and past a large stone water basin beneath the bamboo and

pine trees at the edge of the garden.

Inside the shop there is a trove of fine folk crafts from the fine collection of *mingei* (folk art) furniture pieces owned by the Narita family. The giant wooden pot hook over the open hearth in the center of the main room holds a fine iron *tetsubin* teakettle.

The rough-hewn rafters that support the massive tiled roof are fitted together with complicated Japanese joinery using no nails; the exposed beams were once entirely blackened from the soot that rose from the open hearth below. Many of the houses here share methods of construction used in traditional farmhouses.

It was their pickled *suguki* (*suguki-zuke*) that made the Narita family famous in Kyoto. In 1780, the family started growing *suguki* and pickling them to serve to the priests of Kamigamo Shrine. Then, in 1804, they started selling pickles to restaurants all around Kyoto. About fifteen years ago, when the Kamigamo *shake machi* became a historic preservation district, the Naritas opened a shop to sell their pickles directly to those who had begun to flock here on the weekends. No preservatives are used at Narita. Restaurant owners and housewives as well as tourists

take the extra time required to get to this out-of-the-way location in order to be able to serve Narita pickles at their tables.

Narita also produces a variety of other pickles made from locally grown vegetables in season. But at any time of year you can ask for *kamo-shiba-zuke*, the popular pickles made from eggplant grown only in the fields around the Kamogawa River in this area. The recipe is said to have been handed down from one that belonged to the priests of Kamigamo Shrine. Be sure to wash your *kamo-shiba-zuke* well and squeeze out the excess water before slicing them to serve.

The pickles at Narita are packed in lidded boxes, made of woven sheaths of bamboo, that can be used again and again for packing picnic lunches. Narita employs its own craftsmen to make these boxes, but there are few left who still practice this old craft.

If you wander into the neighborhood on the west side of the Kamogawa to the south of Kamigamo Shrine, you may come across a woman pulling a heavy cart full of vegetables grown in the area. Each vegetable peddler has her own route to follow, stopping at every customer's home for a moment to gossip with the lady of the house along the way. A friend of mine, who lives in a house that is the last stop on the vegetable lady's route, inevitably ends up with whatever she has left over, for free. Ordinarily this works to my friend's advantage, but I'd imagine even the most inventive Kyoto housewife would have trouble dealing with a whole box of leftover burdock root.

SHIOYOSHI-KEN
Kyoto confectionery

In the fall of 1587, the great feudal lord Toyotomi Hideyoshi pulled his gilded boats into port at Yodo to begin his grand procession northward. His residence at Juraku-dai, the "Palace of Gathered Pleasures" that legions of workers had built for him, was located atop the ruins of the old Imperial Palace. Hideyoshi ordered 4,763 loads of earth to be hauled in to construct the mound on which his walled palace stood. Its luxurious gardens were filled with plants requisitioned from the gardens of the local citizenry. The doors of its gates were of solid copper, and the pattern of its roof tiles brought to mind "jeweled tigers breathing in the wind, and golden dragons intoning in the clouds." Hideyoshi had outdone his own reputation as an extravagant showman. But the glory of Juraku-dai was destined to be short-lived. Soon after it was completed Hideyoshi left the palace and his duties as imperial regent to his adopted son to lead an invasion of China. Not ten years later, he ordered the palace to be destroyed when his adopted son's allegiance came under suspicion.

Kyoto confectionery, or *Kyo-gashi*, are known not only for their delicate flavor and imaginative seasonal shapes and colors, but also for the poetic names contrived for each. These often allude to legendary characters, events, or places in Japanese legends or history, or quote memorable passages in literature. *Juraku manju*, a type of sweet bean cake sold at the confectionery shop Shioyoshi-ken, preserves the name of the legendary palace and its

builder. Each bun is branded with "Tencho," the name of the era in which the palace was constructed, and the small cakes are individually wrapped in handmade paper that bears Hideyoshi's family crest, the five-pointed paulownia leaf.

Sweets are an important part of the tea ceremony, and recognition of the particular allusion in the name of the confection offered adds to the pleasure of the gathering. Together with the choice of tea served, the scene depicted on the side of the lacquered tea caddy, the particular flower selected for the arrangement in the *tokonoma* alcove, and the subject of the picture on the hanging scroll, it hints at an unstated scheme on the part of the host.

It is the business of Shioyoshi-ken to indulge the fantasies and tastes of Kyoto's tea masters, a skill it has spent a good hundred years refining. Another of its specialities, the *Kogohigashi*, is named after the beautiful Princess Kogo, an imperial concubine who was banished from the palace when the emperor tired of her. The delicate pink dot on top of each rounded white *Kogo* might lead the ordinary foreigner to imagine that the association is with the young princess's snow-white bosom. Such a rude assumption, though, is heartily denied by, Kenji Takaya, the

TSUKIMOCHI-YA NAOMASA
Kyoto confectionery

fourth-generation master of Shioyoshi-ken; it seems that the cherry-red dot symbolizes the legendary beauty of the princess's tiny mouth. Perhaps the real key to the allusion, even so, is the tiny bit of salty Daitokuji *natto* hidden in the center, which hints at the irony of love, the inevitable shock at finding a teardrop at the heart of an experience so sweet.

Shioyoshi-ken is noted for the wide variety of its confectionery, and the Takaya family prides itself on using only the best available ingredients, including a specially hand-processed sugar called *wasanbon* made at an old-time refinery on Shikoku Island in the Inland Sea. The traditional process by which cane sugar grown on the island is refined produces a powdery white sugar that melts in your mouth.

Such confectionery apart, Shioyoshi-ken is also known for the beauty of its Taisho-period building. The traditional townhouse construction of Shioyoshi-ken has the shop (with family living quarters and interior garden in the rear) on the right side and the kitchens on the left. The porthole-style windows on the second floor overlook a large, wrought-iron gas lantern typical of Kyoto shops dating back to the Meiji or Taisho periods.

Be sure to examine the floral arrangement inside the glass case that lines the wall on the left. Camellias, peonies, plum blossoms, maple leaves, and even wisteria are fashioned out of sugar by Kenji Takaya, Sr. Kenji is a master of *kogei-gashi*, the shaping of floral designs from confectionery, one of Kyoto's more esoteric art forms.

"*Tsukimochi*" means "moon cake"—and the flavor, too, is extraterrestrial. Whether the shop took its name from the small baked bean cakes or vice versa is a question that the years have obscured, for when the first toasted cake was baked on this site five generations ago, neither family, nor bean cake, nor shop had a name. In fact, merchants and artisans in Japan were not allowed to have family names until after 1868, when the Tokugawa shogunate was ousted and the rigid feudal class system officially abolished. People were often known by what they made.

Although the family name is now Kimura, Tsukimochi-ya Naomasa, the shop's formal name, means "Naomasa, the Moon-cake Baker."

It is said that Naomasa invented the type of cake from which he and his shop once took their name. Rather than simply steaming his cakes like ordinary *manju*, Naomasa decided to try placing them in a small clay oven just long enough to give them a light, golden crust. The resulting bean cakes known as *geppei* (or *tsukimochi*) are as tempting to the Western palate as to the Japanese. Another baked specialty of the house, *yaki-guri tsukimochi*, has a chestnut in the center of a *koshi-an* (pureed sweet white bean) filling with the same light crust. A set of five of each kind (the *hitokuchi*, or bite-sized ones, are best) make a mouth-watering souvenir, but should be eaten within a week as no preservatives are added.

Wa-gashi, the general term for Japanese sweets, refers to a wide variety of confectionery that includes *nama-gashi* (jellies, pastes, and doughs), *han-nama-gashi* (steamed, paste-filled buns), *yaki-gashi* (lightly baked cakes, like *tsukimochi*), and *hi-gashi* (sugary wafers). The main ingredients used in all *wa-gashi* are sweet potatoes, chestnuts, red and white beans, brown or white sugar, and rice (or wheat) flour. No animal products (butter, lard, milk) or chocolate are used, and *wa-gashi* are never served as dessert after a meal. They are

snacks to accompany a cup of green tea when guests drop by, or *matcha*, the thick powdered tea of the tea ceremony. Sweets are occasionally served before a meal as appetizers, rather than after dinner, when fruit is considered the appropriate finishing touch.

Tsukimochi-ya also offers a selection of uncooked *nama-gashi* that varies with each of the four seasons. In colors and shapes and with poetic names that evoke spring, winter, summer, and fall, *nama-gashi* decorate the windows at Tsukimochi-ya in turn— delicate doughy peaches, flaky white snowballs, or maple leaves tinted yellow and crimson. *Nama-gashi* can be purchased individually and should be eaten the same day, perhaps with the cup of green tea that awaits visitors at their inn.

The shop, like the delicate sweets it fashions, possesses an air of miniature perfection. Soft light from a Meiji-period glass lamp glows through the stained-glass "moonscape" border on the front window—a decorative touch added around the turn of the century by the flamboyant grandfather of Hironao Kimura, the present owner.

In 1989, Kimura-san was forced to leave his old shop, with its intricate bamboo work and old wooden pantries, to make way for the high-rise building that the owner of the property decided to construct in its place. He tried to build a shop just like the original on property he purchased next door, but city fire ordinances now forbid any new wooden structure downtown. Thus the shop is now in a modern building, but you can still sit inside on a low bamboo bench in Japanese style and watch the owner's mother, now in her late eighties, roll out one by one the sweet cakes you have just ordered.

Note the original shop sign that hangs on the north wall. On the same wall hangs a small painting showing Tsukimochi-ya Naomasa as it was in 1804, when it first went into business—two ladies in kimono, side by side, making bean cakes as the baker slides another paddle-full into the glowing oven. Not much different from today, really—Kimura-san keeps the heart of his special legacy alive.

YUBAHAN

yuba (soy milk "skins")

One brisk autumn morning I was pedaling down a quiet side street, peering into open doorways and exploring new horizons, when I came upon a sight I shall never forget: an old wooden row house whose heavily gridded front windows were open wide to the street, with a crisp linen shop curtain flapping softly in the breeze. It was a scene that had to have come right out of another era.

Hard at work was a man who looked like he was making paper. From steaming vats of an egg-shell-colored liquid, he was pulling dripping wet sheets of what looked like paper and hanging them to dry in the morning air. Walking from vat to vat he repeated the process, once, twice, a dozen times, as rhythmically as a machine but not like a machine, like a man performing a task his bones knew by heart. Steam rose and spun its lazy way up through

the heavy, curved rafters to the skylight twenty feet overhead. In my most polite Japanese, I asked if that wasn't paper he was making. He snorted. "No, it's *yuba*," he said with a grin, knowing where that would leave me. "*Yuba?*" I repeated. He looked at me with amusement, wiped his hands on his apron, and disappeared out back. Soon he returned with a tiny dish and a cruet of soy sauce. "*Yuba*. Try some." I don't remember what else he told me then, if I understood at all. All that lingers is the fragrance of fresh, simmering soy and the memory of my first taste of *yuba*, the pale-yellow soy milk skimmings that look an awful lot like paper—but aren't.

To make *yuba*, soybeans are soaked overnight, ground in a giant stone mortar, and then boiled for hours over an old clay *kamado* stove. Next they are placed in a cheesecloth bag and pressed in an old lever contraption weighted with huge stones that have been in the family for longer than anyone can remember. The extracted soy milk is then placed in long, flat, open vats on the stove. As the vats begin to heat, thin sheets form over the steaming soy milk; they are lifted gently off in one even piece and hung to dry on a wooden stick suspended above.

Yuba can be purchased fresh from the vats (*hikiage yuba*), dried flat (*ita yuba*), or in rolls (*kiri-komaki yuba*). The dried variety lasts a year, but the sooner it is eaten the better. To use dried *yuba*, you simply soak it in hot water or soup until it softens. Sliced and added to soups, it absorbs the flavor of any seasoning. Since it contains the highest concentration of protein found in any natural food, *yuba* is an important part of *shojin ryori*, the Buddhist vegetarian cuisine.

When I returned to Yubahan several years later, the man and his wonderful old shop hadn't changed—but I had. I'd tasted the popular Kyoto specialty a hundred times in the soups and subtle sauces of Kyoto-style cuisine.

He dusted off a spot for me to sit amid the stone grinding mortars, the giant wooden tubs, and the old clay *kamado* and went on with his work. (I was there this time for an interview, but boiling soy milk waits for no woman.) Each sheet of *yuba* takes eight to ten minutes to form; no clocks or timers

are involved, just one continuous motion of lifting, hanging, and moving on to the next vat, all day long. When I commented on the difficulty of keeping an age-old tradition like this going, he—Tomizo Asano, the ninth-generation *yuba* maker—brushed it off with a laugh. "It's no big deal, I've been making *yuba* since I was thirteen years old. It's just what I do," he said.

Yubahan started making *yuba* in 1716, but all family records were destroyed in the huge fire that destroyed much of the city in 1864, a result of the battles that took place at the time of the Meiji Restoration. The 120-year-old building was reconstructed not long after the fire, but apart from that, little is left of the shop's history besides hand-me-down tales.

Lifting yet another sheet of *yuba* onto a rack to dry, Asano-san gave a nonchalant grin when I asked why his shop's name, "Yubahan," is written with Chinese characters meaning "half a wave of hot water," rather than with the usual characters for *yuba*. "Who knows?" he said. "I guess that's a question I never got around to asking Dad."

SECTION III

RESTAURANTS & INNS

Restaurants

AZEKURA   *soba* noodles

HIRANO-YA   *ayu* (sweet fish)

MINOKO   *cha-kaiseki* cuisine

MISOKA-AN KAWAMICHI-YA   *soba* noodles

NASAKURA-RO   restaurant

NISHIKI   *kaiseki* cuisine

TAKASEBUNE   tempura

KASAGI-YA   sweets and tea

ICHIWA   rice cakes

BUNNOSUKE-JAYA *amazake*

Inns (Ryokan)

HIIRAGI-JAYA   inn, restaurant

HIIRAGI-YA   inn

TAWARA-YA   inn

KINMATA   inn, restaurant

KIKAKU-TEI   inn, restaurant

AZEKURA

soba noodles

Not far from Kamigamo-jinja, on the old road that leads to Midoroga-ike Pond, there is a three-hundred-year-old saké warehouse that was saved from the jaws of progress twenty years ago by a very thoughtful kimono merchant named Mikio Ichida. More amazing than the salvation of the building itself is that it used to stand over forty kilometers to the southeast, in Nara, where the Kintetsu Train Station is now located. Ichida-san had the enormous structure dismantled piece by piece, brought to Kyoto, and rebuilt on the estate of a former samurai family called Okamoto, one of the oldest *shake* (priest families) of Kamigamo Shrine.

The building is a marvel of Japanese joinery, as a glance up at the massive rough-hewn rafters or the cypress crossbeams that support the heavy tile roof high above will tell. This giant *kura* belonged originally to a saké brewery called "Kikuya," built during the early Edo period in Nara, southeast of Kyoto. Buildings like this are no longer common because of the scarcity of timber this size in Japan and the decreasing number of carpenters skilled in this type of construction. It took nearly a year to complete the move; every beam and crosspost was fitted together as it was originally—the complicated joinery hasn't a single nail.

With a few modifications to the interior, the 1,250-square-meter *kura* now serves homemade *soba* noodles in the main room, which has been decorated in Japanese folk-style. It also hosts exhibitions of kimono and *ikebana* periodically in the spacious tatami room upstairs. Whether you take a stool at a low wooden table or sit on tatami beside the open hearth (*irori*), lunch at Azekura at any time of the year is a comfortable, country-style experience. Through the kitchen window, you can watch as the cook rolls out the buckwheat dough and slices it into noodles by hand. The restaurant overlooks a rustic garden complete with churning waterwheel. After lunch you can stroll through the grounds for a look at the tea-house, set amidst a grove of bamboo on the hillside at the back of the estate, or visit the little museum across the courtyard from the main *kura*. It houses a collection of

old brewery equipment, tools, and furniture.

The name Azekura is written with characters that express the owner's appreciation of fine textiles —*A*, love; *ze*, dyeing; *kura*, storehouse. Though many of the textile exhibitions in the main building are trade shows not open to the public, you can peek inside the Hida House, a building on the grounds that is a reconstruction of a country house from the Hida-Takayama District, and watch the group of weavers at work on their hand looms.

Between Kamigamo Shrine and Azekura there is another, smaller shrine called Ota-jinja. Except for a few weeks in mid-May when the irises are in bloom in the pond beside it, this is a quiet place. Surrounded by towering cypresses some twenty meters high, it has the sense of being in the midst of nature that is characteristic of Shinto shrines. Even atop office buildings in midtown, you'll find that shrines housing the company's protective divinity are seldom without a backdrop of greenery.

Such Shinto shrines are often dedicated to a particular deity, such as the gods of fire, thunder, or harvest.

Shrines are also used as focal points for the community, each having a festival that brings the neighborhood together at least once a year. Dedicated to Ame-no-uzume-no-mikoto, the god of good harvest, Ota-jinja has been in the hands of the priests and parishioners of Kamigamo Shrine since the twelfth century, and the love of generations of parishioners is evident each year in late spring, when hundreds of carefully tended purple and yellow irises make their appearance just as they have for centuries. The exact origin of Ota-jinja is unrecorded, but over the centuries people have come here to pray not only for a good harvest, but for protection against illness, for good luck in marriage, and even for a successful career on the stage. As with most Shinto shrines, Ota-jinja has a long list of talented deities who can be enlisted to help out in almost any difficult situation.

By far the most frequent visitors are the children. The last and perhaps most important function of the guardian spirit of a neighborhood shrine is to provide children with a safe and beautiful place to play. The woods make splendid hiding places, and Ota-jinja is seldom without its band of little people laughing and running beneath the sacred cypresses.

HIRANO-YA
ayu (sweet fish)

Smoke twists and rises above the thatched rooftops in a country village at sunset. Below, the light of the bath fires glows in the darkness. A single cricket perseveres on the edge of winter, the sound of footsteps warning him to be silent—he is, after all, alone now. Steep-sloped mountains cradle the ancient valley and the last few farmers trudge home from their rice fields, another year's work almost done.

Sagano in the western part of Kyoto was once nothing more (or less) than a quiet country village; today, though, there is hardly a scrap of countryside within the city limits of Kyoto left untouched by urban sprawl. Sagano is perhaps the last area in which vestiges of rice fields and farmhouses, once common along the outskirts of Kyoto, can still be found at all.

Just inside the vermilion *torii* gate that leads up the mountainside to Atago Shrine on the northwest edge of Sagano stands a four-hundred-year-old thatched teahouse called Hirano-ya. Grilled *ayu*, a small freshwater fish popular in Kyoto, is the specialty of the house now, but long ago a cup of tea and a skewer of *shinko dango*, a popular local rice confection, were the treats for which Hirano-ya was known. For centuries, its homemade *dango* provided shrine worshippers with the encouragement to tackle the steep, two-hour climb to the top of Atago-san, the mountain on which dwells the god who puts out fires.

Fire has always been the most dreaded affliction in Kyoto, and it became customary for citizens to climb the hill once a month to plead for mercy from the cantankerous God of Fire. Though this custom has given way to a once-a-year symbolic climb in July, the pair of old teahouses at the base of the hill beside the *torii* still offer rest and nourishment to faithful worshippers and to anyone who enjoys *ayu* served in gracious traditional country style.

The *ayu* served at Hirano-ya are caught in the nearby Hozugawa River, brought live by local fishermen, and placed in the large pond out back. No refrigerator is used, so each morning just enough fish are caught from the pond to last the day, a process you can watch from the open veranda where you'll

be seated overlooking not only the pond, but a backdrop of maple trees whose tiny star-shaped leaves form a jigsaw puzzle against the sky.

Hirano-ya's *ayu* meal served in formal *kaiseki* style is expensive. But the smell of freshly caught fish grilling over charcoal in the kitchen below and the rustic beauty of this two-hundred-year-old farmhouse are just about the only tastes of traditional Japanese countryside to be had this side of Mt. Atago. *Ayu* season is from May through October, and in the fall the *yudofu-no-okimari* lunch of tofu simmered in a ceramic pot at your table is priced very reasonably. For a brief country pause, the original *shinko dango* are still made fresh every morning and served with green tea at prices even pilgrims can afford.

The unusual Saga paper lanterns that light each room at Hirano-ya are a special source of pride for Tamiko Inoue, the thirteenth-generation proprietress of the old restaurant. It is difficult to find rustic lanterns like these; she must order them from the last craftsman in the area who still knows how to weave the bamboo spines and coat the handmade paper with tannin the way they were made in the old days. Giant and asymmetrical, they glow with a soft amber light that sets the mood at Hirano-ya, a quality described in Japanese as *soboku*, the artless beauty of things that belong to the countryside.

Kyoto Prefecture includes miles and miles of breathtaking farmland that stretches all the way to the Japan Sea. After lunch under the thatched roofs of the old teahouse, a short drive through the tunnel to the west will lead you to Kiyotaki, a country village from which you can begin a hike that leads along the banks of a river and into the hills beyond. Or drive up through the Takao Parkway to Highway 162 which, in three hours, will take you down winding mountain roads to the Japan Sea. Valleys wedged between steep cedar-covered mountains reveal tiny farm villages around every bend, scenes not long for this rapidly urbanizing world.

MINOKO
cha-kaiseki cuisine

Just below the stone *torii* gate on the south side of Yasaka Shrine lies Shimogawara-cho, a quiet neighborhood of innkeepers and restaurateurs that forms the eastern fringe of Gion, the old pleasure quarter of Kyoto. A stroll down the narrow cobblestone path called Ishibe-koji, with its high rock walls and impressive old villas, might suggest an exclusive residential district belonging to the privileged few. Many of these fine structures were indeed the villas of wealthy Kyoto merchants, but after World War II, when many families lost their fortunes, several of the residences were turned into inns or "teahouses" (*o-chaya*) and now cater

professionally to the same class of people that once inhabited them.

Nowadays the area, like Gion, comes alive only after dark. While retaining the dignity of former days, the teahouses and inns of Shimogawara-cho now have the added hint of intrigue that surrounds the world of the geisha, who are frequently called here to entertain.

Just before the narrow alley that leads to Ishibe-koji, you'll encounter one of these former villas, a *ryotei* called Minoko that has combined the world of Gion with another dimension in its elegant *cha-kaiseki*: the delicate meal served at formal tea-ceremony gatherings.

Cha-kaiseki differs from ordinary *kaiseki* not only in the characters that form the name, but in both purpose and style. The *kai* means pocket or fold, and the *seki* means stone, a reference to the heated stones that Zen priests placed inside the folds of their garments to warm their bellies against the chill of unheated temples in winter. The *cha* means tea, and the meal served with the tea ceremony is intended to be "just enough to keep you warm," a reference to the self-discipline and restraint that are among the ideals of both Zen and the Way of Tea.

Cha-kaiseki, as served in conjunction with the tea ceremony, is a highly formal affair. At Minoko you have the chance to experience the same meal in a more relaxed atmosphere—served with a bowl of thick green tea in a setting with all the natural beauty and simple elegance of a formal tearoom, but without the strain of the accompanying ceremony and its complicated etiquette.

At lunchtime Minoko serves an informal box lunch called *chabako-bento* after the lacquered container in which it is served, and resembling the boxes that are used to carry utensils to outdoor tea gatherings. Luncheon guests are served in a spacious tatami room overlooking a tea garden with stone lanterns and the sound of trickling water from a stream.

In the evening, by reservation only, guests are seated in private tearooms with a view of the same lovely garden and are served in the height of *cha-kaiseki* style. One course after another of carefully arranged seasonal delicacies arrives on square porcelain

trays, bamboo platters, and lacquered bowls chosen to complement the mood of the season.

So careful is the owner, Kojiro Yoshida, about the seasonal appropriateness of items on each evening's menu that eggs, for example, are never served at Minoko during the hot summer months. "A difficult time for the chickens," as he puts it.

As we discussed the fine points of the four seasons over tea, a turtle sat sunning himself on a rock beside the stone lantern outside. It seems we were not the only ones enjoying that moment of tranquility at Minoko.

MISOKA-AN KAWAMICHI-YA
soba noodles

Acrobatics may not be a prominent tradition in Japan, but the Kyoto delivery boy on a bicycle who frantically dodges taxicabs, buses, and pedestrians with a tray overflowing with steaming bowls of *soba* noodles balanced on one shoulder is the next best thing.

Soba, or buckwheat noodles served in a variety of soups, are found everywhere—on train-station platforms, next door to movie houses, down the street or around the corner in everybody's neighborhood. And they can range in flavor from dishwater to delicacy. But connoisseurs in Kyoto frequent the two or three old *soba* shops that have survived several generations of discriminating customers by continuing to serve the finest homemade buckwheat noodles and broth.

Kawamichi-ya is one of the best. Not far from the center of town, it serves a wide variety of noodle dishes in a shop that is as wonderful as the menu in English. It is difficult to tell whether Kawamichi-ya is in a garden, or vice versa. The long, narrow Kyoto-style building has three gardens, all to assure that you are surrounded by greenery in any season: a front garden with a beautiful plum tree that drapes its blossom-laden branches over the gateway in spring, a central courtyard garden with tables where you may sit outside if the weather permits, and a quiet garden that surrounds the small open-air room at the back.

Light streams in through the windows to catch the sheen of polished wood in the interior—in midwinter, a hanging scroll depicts a crow huddled on a snowy branch; a flower arrangement of graceful pampas grass heralds early fall; the sound of a tiny porcelain wind chime catches the slightest breeze on a sultry August afternoon.

Upstairs, there are private tatami rooms overlooking the tile rooftops of midtown, but the downstairs area with its stone lanterns, interior gardens, and the aroma of broth simmering in the nearby kitchen is the place most regular customers prefer.

The tradition of *soba* noodles in Japan dates

back to the early seventeenth century, and Kawami-chi-ya traces its own history to a time some three hundred years ago when it provided noodles to pilgrims climbing Mt. Hiei to pray at Enryaku-ji, the great Tendai Buddhist temple at the top. Every year on May 16, the birthday of Emperor Kanmu, who founded the city of Kyoto, the people at Kawamichi-ya set up stalls on top of the holy mountain, serving *soba* to worshippers who climb the steep slopes to attend memorial services. The Emperor Kanmu gave aid of some forgotten nature to the ancestors of the Kawamichi-ya family way back in the ninth century, and even now, their descendants have not forgotten to thank him each year with this special service in his memory.

In the old days, noodles were something to be eaten, if not actually cooked at home, so Kawamichi-ya's delivery boys have been practicing their back-street acrobatics for as long as there have been bicycles in Kyoto.

The specialty at Kawamichi-ya is a one-pot noodle dish called *hokoro* that is prepared over a burner at your table in handcrafted Mongolian hot pots.

The establishment also makes tasty buckwheat cookies, for which it is famous. During the Meiji period, when confectionery shared in the vogue for all things Western across Japan, Kawamichi-ya came across a great Portuguese recipe, brought to Japan in the sixteenth century, for a cookie that they later named *boro*. The word *boro* is thought to come from the Portuguese *bola*, meaning "ball," though, true to Kyoto form, the famed old shop makes them in the shape of plum blossoms instead. The cookie shop, built in the late Edo period, is located around the corner from the noodle shop.

Just inside the rope curtains that separate the kitchen from the shop you'll find another of the secrets to Kawamichi-ya's long success—a row of figurines of round-bellied, grinning Hotei, the guardian deity of traditional Kyoto kitchens. Only a few of the original set of fifteen are on display above the old cookstove in the shop; the remainder have been relegated in recent years to a niche on the wall of a new garage across the street. Perhaps the gods will learn to adapt to their new, if less glamorous, role of guarding delivery trucks.

中村樓

NAKAMURA-RO
restaurant

Standing on the bridge at Shijo I see a light:
Is it Yasaka Shrine… or can it be the lanterns
of Niken-jaya?

> Anonymous

Nobody remembers how long people have been stopping for a cup of tea and a bite of tofu beside the stone *torii* gate at Yasaka Shrine in Gion. But the pair of teahouses known as Niken-jaya were famous by the end of the sixteenth century. Today only one has survived—Nakamura-ro, said to be the oldest restaurant in Japan. Rather than tearing down the tiny one-room hut that made them famous, Masamitsu Tsuji, the twelfth-generation owner of what is now a luxurious restaurant and inn next door, guards the humble teahouse as a precious family heirloom.

Sliding open the *shoji* paper doors in midwinter, you become part of a world that no longer exists anywhere else. A worn stone floor, a wood-burning clay stove called a *kamado* with a sputtering kettle of water on for tea, the rough-hewn stone tofu basins, the charcoal grill for heating the skewers of tofu, a stone well so deep you cannot see the bottom, its lid so heavy that no one lifts it anymore, and a pair of imperturbable ladies in kimono who seem to be part of the same comfortable time warp.

In summertime, the doors disappear completely, opening onto the graveled walkway to the shrine, looking much as it does in an old Edo-period woodblock print, with pilgrims and foreigners, itinerant priests and small dogs gathered around waiting for their order of tofu *dengaku* (skewers of tofu covered with miso sauce) to be placed on the low benches before them. Foreign visitors have been coming to the popular teahouse since before the Edo period, and a bowl of *o-usu* (the powdered tea of the tea ceremony), and a dish of tofu *dengaku* still make just as fine an afternoon snack as they did of old.

Late in the nineteenth century an inn and formal restaurant were built beside the teahouse to accommodate the number of daimyo (feudal lords) who flocked to Kyoto, which had become the focal point of a struggle to overthrow the shogunate and reinstate the emperor as ruler of Japan. The tales of clandestine meetings among plotters on both sides, held in the banquet rooms and parlors of Nakamura-ro, are easy to imagine as you walk down the long, narrow corridors that lead up and down stairways to the inner recesses of the inn. One regally appointed room at the back of the inn, now famous for its screen paintings by Korin Ogata, was once the temporary residence of Arisugawa-no-miya, brother of Emperor Meiji.

All the rooms overlook a magnificent central garden that always has flowers in season: cherry trees in springtime, followed by azaleas, hydrangeas, chrysanthemums, and camellias. The inn still serves as a quiet retreat for the poets and writers who have been making annual pilgrimages to Nakamura-ro for decades.

One of Masamitsu Tsuji's relatives owns Tsujitome, the most famous *kaiseki* caterer in Kyoto. Shigemitsu Tsuji, Masamitsu's late father, was the author of an authoritative volume on tofu cuisine. The cuisine at Nakamura-ro is strictly Kyoto-style. Tsuji-san believes that the natural flavor of the ingredients is the secret to fine cooking, and he uses much less salt, sugar, soy sauce, and spice than do chefs in other regions of Japan. Kyoto cooking is acknowledged to be the most delicately seasoned in the country.

In Kyoto today, the younger generation often sets about modernizing the venerable legacies of its parents. When Masamitsu's father passed away some years ago, mourners who attended the funeral, many of them old customers, implored the young son not to change a thing in the cherished old inn. Masamitsu Tsuji, much to their delight, was only too happy to oblige.

NISHIKI

kaiseki cuisine

Some years ago, not long before she passed away, I had the pleasure of meeting Ine Tanaka. At 91, she was one of the heartiest spirits I've ever had the pleasure to meet. For over forty years she had been the proprietress of one of Kyoto's most popular restaurants, and the story of her life was every bit as amazing as her *kaiseki* menu was— and still is—delicious.

"Actually, I was born in Tokyo," she told me, "so people around here consider me kind of a foreigner. I married a man whose family owned a pair of tempura restaurants, one on the Ginza and another in Osaka. He threw me out when I didn't bear him any children. That's the way it was in those days—the man's word was law. I had no choice but to leave.

"I ended up staying in Osaka with his folks, no less, to help them manage their restaurant. As could be expected, we didn't get along, and when I asked them if they'd consider selling the place to me, I think they agreed just to get rid of me. They wanted ¥3,000, which was a fortune before the war. I rounded up ten regular customers and talked them into loaning me ¥300 each. In no time my place was one of the best tempura restaurants around ... until the bombings, that is. The place burnt to the ground, and I decided it was time to move to a quieter town.

"I wound up staying at a rundown old inn in Kyoto out on a sandbar in the middle of the river in Arashiyama. The old couple who owned it were looking for someone to take it off their hands, so I volunteered. (I had to borrow the money again, mind you.) Little by little I pulled the place together and opened another restaurant right here. I named it Nishiki," she grinned ironically. "The same as my ex-husband's place in Tokyo!"

When I first visited Nishiki, Ine Tanaka was still bustling around the corridors every day, bowing to customers and barking orders at the maids to straighten the shoes the guests had left in a jumble by the door. "You have to be on them every minute," she whispered again. "That's the only way to be sure the place is run the way you want it." In the kitchen, a dozen young cooks scurried back and

forth worriedly as the tiny, gray-haired rear-admiral-in-kimono scrutinized the *sashimi* slicing. In a restaurant serving three hundred people a day, there is no time for mistakes.

The one-hundred-year-old inn has been remodeled, but the traditional tatami rooms perch out over the Oi River on the southern side of the sandbar just as they always have. This area is part of a historic preservation district now, so the rooms at Nishiki sprawl low along the river bank, half hidden behind the high bamboo fence that, in keeping with the local style, surrounds the entire place. Reservations are a must, though you may have a chance without them if you arrive before 11 A.M. (and if it's not spring or fall, when the scenery of Arashiyama is a riot of maple leaves and tourists).

The menu is *kaiseki* style with all the delicate courses, but presented in an old-fashioned workman's lacquered lunch box with drawers. Thus the meal, called *o-shuku-zen*, is an eclectic cross between formal *kaiseki* and a deluxe *bento* box lunch.

The basic seven-course *o-shuku-zen* is one of the most reasonably priced in town for a *kaiseki*-style meal of such quality and proportions. Every month the ingredients are changed completely to match the season, and Tanaka-san's son prepares a special booklet every month, describing in exact detail each course to be served, for customers to peruse while they are waiting.

A sample menu for the month of July featured such seasonal treats as *ayu no shio-yaki*, small freshwater white fish, salted and grilled; *karashi-dofu*, a spicy local tofu dish; and *age-nasubi*, fried eggplant in miso sauce, served in a silver eggplant-shaped container.

Nishiki has become a popular afternoon spot, particularly with women—this is a city where restaurants were once the exclusive domain of men. Thinking over Ine Tanaka's amazing life, I asked her one last question—what did she think about "women's lib"?

"'Women's lib?'" she cackled. "Good heavens, dear, I'm an old lady … what would I know about a thing like that!"

TAKASEBUNE
tempura

Today the Kamogawa river runs calmly through the middle of Kyoto like a trusted old friend, but in its youth it was known to have a definite mean streak. In the old days it stormed through town, drowning citizens and destroying homes and shops with a vengeance—always unexpected, always devastating. But the city forgave it each time, like a helpless parent with an intractable child. Then one day in the early seventeenth century, a wealthy merchant named Ryoi Suminokura, who ran a very profitable shipping trade to ports in Southeast Asia, decided to teach the spoiled child a lesson. With permission from the shogun, he dug a canal that drained the river of its surplus energy and enabled his boatmen to carry their loads to Fushimi and on to the port city of Osaka in the south without further harassment.

The Takasegawa canal runs along the western edge of the Kamogawa all the way to Fushimi, where it joins the Yodo River. Until the late nine-teenth century, boatmen plied their long flatboats up and down the canal, carrying firewood, charcoal, rice, salt, saké, and prisoners being sent to exile. The area embracing the canal between Nijo and Gojo is known as Kiyamachi; once the home of charcoal and firewood merchants, it is now the center of a glittery entertainment district filled with restaurants, bars, and hostess clubs—with a few old restaurants and inns tucked in among them.

When modern transportation came to Kyoto around the turn of the century in the form of street-cars and trains, the backbreaking job of operating the boats on the Takasegawa became obsolete. Carrying merchandise downstream was not such an arduous task, but the boatmen had to drag the heavy barges back up the river using poles and ropes that they manipulated from the banks of the canal.

When Shotaro Okajima opened his restaurant on the west bank of the canal thirty years ago, he named it Takasebune, after the flatboats his father

once pulled up that same river. Takasebune is a small family place that has become famous for its *tempura teishoku*, a table d'hote tempura dinner that includes a generous bowl of miso soup, rice, and pickles, along with a basket of crisply fried tempura shrimp, fish, and vegetables. The amazing thing about Takasebune's tempura meal is that it is delicious and inexpensive at the same time.

Apart from the lunch menu, Takasebune specializes in a variety of fine fish dishes, with a new menu penned each night by Okajima-san himself. He is a handsome gentleman with a full head of snow-white hair and an endearing gruffness. He and his soft-spoken son will seat you at the counter, where you can watch all the culinary activity, though private tatami rooms are available upstairs and in back. Okajima-san knows his fish, which is bought fresh daily at a market just blocks away. His grandfather ran a small shop on the same site after retiring from his job as a Takasegawa boatman. An old photograph of him and his boat hangs just inside the entrance.

When they opened their restaurant, identified by the boat oar that leans against the side of the building out front, the Okajimas decided to offer the local working people a decent midday meal of tempura at a reasonable price. That's the spirit of Takasebune: even the deluxe full-course dinners served in the evening are not geared to earn them a fortune.

On the short *noren* curtain that hangs above the counter, there is an inscription in calligraphy that reads, "Came down the river through Kyoto on a boat, just me and the cows." The haiku poet Akamatsu Ryushi wrote the message—a pun about the owner having been born in the Year of the Cow. Somehow it sets the mood of the whole place.

かさぎ屋

KASAGI-YA
sweets and tea

Amato no sudori dekinai Ninenzaka
Ninenzaka, the sweet-lover's downfall.
  by the poet Tenmin, on the wall at Kasagi-ya

The copper kettle sputters over the hibachi coals. With ease and elegance, the proprietor, kimono sleeves tucked into his *obi* sash, whisks a bowl of *o-usu*, thick green tea, to a froth. Carrying it gracefully across the tiny room with its sagging stone floor, he turns the bowl clockwise so that the *shomen*, or "face," is directed toward his guest and places it on the table with a full bow, just as the host might at a formal tea ceremony. Although Kasagi-ya is not a formal tearoom, the graciousness and hospitality that are the essence of tea are carried on here—quietly, lovingly, and in the spirit of humility that Sen no Rikyu sought to evoke in his *wabi-cha*, the aesthetic of unaffected refinement.

When asked about which school of tea he attended, Hirozo Hayakawa seemed hesitant to reply. "Well, Omote-senke, the so-called aristocratic Way of Tea … but I stopped all that years ago," he said. "What I do here isn't really tea ceremony at all. I just serve tea and sweets the way I think is best." He walked over to light another chip of natural sandalwood in an incense burner in the corner.

His wife supervises the kitchen in back, where she and her daughter make fresh *o-hagi* every morning. *O-hagi* is a very homey Japanese sweet made with a sticky rice center and a coating of sweet red adzuki beans (or vice versa.) *O-hagi* was originally served during the celebration of the autumn equinox, and the name comes from a willowy bush clover that flowers only in the fall. At Kasagi-ya, Mrs. Toshie Hayakawa makes the *o-hagi* fresh while you wait and serves them still warm, a rare treat in Kyoto today. They are sweet (but not overwhelmingly), a complement to the astringent flavor of *o-usu*. One 94-year-old *o-hagi* addict in Kyoto told me they're the best she's ever had.

Kasagi-ya is located at the foot of the steps running from Ninenzaka to Sannenzaka, the cobbled paths that lead up the hill to Kiyomizu Temple, one of the most famous in Japan. The tiny, one-room shop seats no more than ten people and

has been serving refreshments to visitors to the temple since 1914.

The sloping, stone-paved lanes that lead up to Kiyomizu-dera have been worn smooth over the centuries by the constant flow of pilgrims to the great temple dedicated to Kannon, the Goddess of Mercy. A little over a decade ago, this neighborhood was designated a historic preservation district. Its many ceramics shops, antique shops, and inns make the area a mecca for tourists.

One of the most noted turn-of-the-century customers at Kasagi-ya was a Taisho-period painter named Takehisa Yumeji (1884–1934), whose female portraits are said to show the frail woman he lived with in the old house next door to Kasagi-ya. A victim of tuberculosis, she died young, leaving Takehisa haunted by the memory of her fragile beauty. One of Takehisa's rare landscape scenes hangs on the wall to the left of the entrance.

Aside from *o-usu* and *o-hagi*, Kasagi-ya serves other sweets and beverages to complement the season, such as *o-shiruko*, a smooth sweet bean soup, and *zenzai*, whole sweet red beans in a light broth, both popular in winter, and *kori-mizore*, shaved ice with sweet syrup on top, and *kori-uji*, shaved ice with green tea syrup on top, in summer.

The interior of Kasagi-ya, with its antique light fixtures, its old wooden tobacco boxes, wicker stools, and *senja-fuda* (stickers bearing the names of former visitors, some of them famous actors and artists), is one of the only places in this area that has not been tampered with. While other shops have completely remodeled to accommodate the throngs of tourists who flock to soak up the atmosphere of "old Kyoto," Kasagi-ya quietly retains what its shinier neighbors lack: genuine warmth and hospitality.

いち和

ICHIWA
rice cakes

Mochi wa mochiya
Leave rice cakes to the rice-cake maker.

"Old" is a relative term. Two hundred years is about as old as you can get in America; a thousand years is "pretty old" in Japan. Ichiwa, a shop that has served grilled *mochi* (rice cakes) in sweet sauce to visitors to Imamiya Shrine since the Heian period, is "pretty old" by any standard.

Mrs. Hasegawa, at 83, is old too, but doesn't seem to mind. She bustles back and forth between her wood-burning cookstove in back and the charcoal grill out front, endlessly turning the little skewers of *aburi-mochi* in winter snow or summer thunderstorm, just as she has all her life. "*Binbo wa hima nashi* (the poor have no time to spare)," says Mrs. Hasegawa as she rushes out, wiping her hands on her apron, to welcome customers with a hearty "*O-koshi-yasu*" and usher them into a seat beside the little garden in back, which (according to family legend) was designed by Kobori Enshu, the famous seventeenth-century tea master and landscape garden designer. Even the tea-caddy-shaped stone water basin in the old garden attests to Ichiwa's long association with the masters of tea. The crystal-clear water, drawn from the ancient well at the center of the shop, has been sought after by tea people for centuries, and the daughter of the grand master of Urasenke, the world-famous school of tea, is even rumored to have a secret sweet tooth when it comes to Mrs. Hasegawa's tasty *aburi-mochi*.

Aburi-mochi are cakes of rice-flour dough, charcoal grilled and dipped in sweet miso. The bamboo skewers on which the *mochi* is placed for grilling are split by hand from green bamboo stalks, a task that fills spare moments at Ichiwa. Sixteen skewers are used with every serving, so it keeps the Hasegawas busy all the time.

Aburi-mochi has connections with a very old festival that is held at the Imamiya Shrine, outside

whose gates Ichiwa has stood for centuries. Yasurai Matsuri, celebrated at the shrine on the first Sunday in April, dates to an eleventh-century epidemic that took the lives of thousands. Records state that the death toll was so high that bodies had to be carried twenty-five miles to the south to be cast into the Inland Sea. The festival was intended to pacify the unhappy spirits of the fallen cherry blossoms, which were thought to have caused the epidemic. Dressed in red and black wigs representing demons, the participants beat drums and chant "Flowers, rest in peace!" with great emphasis.

Apart from this ritual, *sekihan*—rice cooked with red adzuki beans and served at festive occasions throughout Japan (in this case with flower petals on top)—and skewers of *aburi-mochi* were said to be all that was needed to ward off disease till the following year. Ichiwa sells *aburi-mochi* every day of the year now, but their history is tied to that of this ancient shrine.

Even apart from the thousand years of history and the chance to sit in this wonderful three-hundred-year-old building and taste the delicious sweet *mochi*, Mrs. Hasegawa herself is worth the trip to the shop standing north of Daitoku-ji temple, one of the oldest and most famous Zen temples in Japan.

When I asked her about the equally old and marvelous *aburi-mochi* shop, Kasuragi, just across the way, she whispered, "Yes, they're very old too, but the shop changed hands not long ago" (two hundred years ago, to be exact), as if she were letting us in on a recent neighborhood scandal. She is justifiably proud of her twenty-three-generation heritage, and her daughter and granddaughter work beside her every day, reassuring her that, unlike some of the other old shops in Kyoto, Ichiwa has a future.

文の助茶屋

BUNNOSUKE-JAYA
amazake (a sweet beverage)

Sute Yamada, at age 84, carries on today with an entrepreneur's gusto the family business of selling *amazake* (reportedly the favorite drink of Buddhist nuns) left to her and her late husband by his father, the noted *rakugo* artist whose stage name was Bunnosuke Katsura. *Rakugo* is the Japanese art of storytelling—funny, often bawdy storytelling—and one look at the shop and the profusion of knickknacks and memorabilia hanging from every inch of ceiling and crowding every shelf conveys the essence of the whole tradition.

The popularity of *rakugo* began to decline around the turn of the century: rickshaws went out with the advent of roadsters, *rakugo* went out with talking pictures. By the end of the Meiji period, Bunnosuke had had enough of empty theaters and decided to spend an early retirement refurbishing a run-down *amazake* shop that seemed to have been fighting a similar battle for survival.

There were once scores of *amazake* shops in this area about midway between Yasaka Shrine and Kiyomizu Temple. *Amazake* is a sweet drink made from saké lees and served hot. Though it has the aroma of the "real thing," it contains no alcohol and is said to have been the invention of Buddhist nuns. Kodai-ji, a nunnery just across the road from Bunnosuke-jaya, may be the reason this one *amazake* shop still exists at all.

Beautifully restored and opened to the public a few years ago, Kodai-ji is one of Kyoto's best-kept secrets. It was founded in 1606 after the death of the great military leader Toyotomi Hideyoshi, when his grief-stricken widow vowed to enter a nunnery. Perhaps out of remorse, Hideyoshi's successor, Tokugawa Ieyasu, presented her with Kodai-ji, and she lived out her life in its cloistered halls. He even

ordered that the So-mon Gate of Hideyoshi's Fushimi castle be moved there to comfort her. Not ten years later Ieyasu was to wipe out every last member of the Toyotomi line.

Entoku-in, to the south of Bunnosuke-jaya,

was the house of Hideyoshi's younger brother, Kinoshita Toshifusa, and the gate that still stands before it is typical of the *yashiki*, or samurai dwellings, of the sixteenth century. There is a teahouse, and a garden designed by the famous tea master and landscape architect Kobori Enshu using stones from Hideyoshi's Momoyama castle, destroyed by Ieyasu in 1620.

At the back of Bunnosuke-jaya is a small shrine to Daikoku-ten, the god of wealth (and one of the seven gods of good luck so popular in Japan). Daikoku-ten was Hideyoshi's patron saint, and his widow is said to have brought the jolly deity with her to this site from Osaka Castle. Daikoku-ten, who is also the patron saint of farmers, is often depicted sitting on top of two large bales of rice, but he is so open-handed with his treasures, symbolized by the giant sack full of treasures on his back, that the rat who nibbles at his rice bales is in fact a beloved friend.

From the low benches outdoors under the awning, where *amazake* or *matcha* (the thick tea of the tea ceremony) is served, there is a full view of one of the most bizarre collections of art and trivia in Japan. Note the photo of old Bunnosuke and his wife, taken in the Meiji period, for a glimpse at the flamboyant character behind this whole affair. This eclectic spot seems more like an event than a tea shop. Opposite the kitchen, occupying a place of honor above the door to the storage-room, is a woodblock print that Yamada-san insists is by Hokusai. Tucked away amidst the old clocks, chests, tobacco boxes, kites, and folk dolls collected by Yamada-san's husband on many train trips around the countryside, there are even several interesting samples of Japanese folk erotica. If asked about them, her late husband would bring them out. With a teasing, roguish grin, he would place a foot-long lingam as wide as a cannon barrel in the hands of an unsuspecting young lady sipping her sweet drink on his porch. "How about this?" he would ask, anticipating the giggles with glee.

Much of Mr. Yamada's time was spent in the back room with his TV set and his beloved albums full of photos of Tamasaburo, one of his favorite kabuki actors and a good friend. It took a good deal of cajoling to persuade him to come out and tell stories, but when the gaunt old fellow in his somber, striped kimono begrudgingly sat himself on a *zabuton* cushion on the tatami mats out front, and, after adjusting his tobacco box and lighting a long-stemmed *kiseru* pipe, he finally began, you'd swear that *rakugo* was something in the blood.

HEIHACHI-JAYA
inn (ryokan), restaurant

Four hundred years ago, footsore fish peddlers returning to Kyoto after the twenty-four-hour trek from the Japan Sea were relieved to find Heihachi-jaya just where they'd left it at the foot of the mountains, welcoming them home with tea, barley rice, and a place to rest their loads.

Heihachi-jaya still offers weary travelers the same promise of comfort and a good meal. Hugging the east bank of the Takano River, the old road-house on the northeastern outskirts of Kyoto is now an inn and restaurant serving *kaiseki*-style freshwater fish cuisine and the barley rice and tea for which it was known centuries ago. Entering the moss-covered Kigyumon Gate, which once belonged to a rural Zen temple, you leave the city behind and stroll through a lush garden into a quiet world that seems to belong to a different time.

During the Edo period this inn was the popular haunt of samurai and wealthy merchants, who knew of the inn's reputation for the best fish cuisine in the capital. Yamabana Heihachi-jaya, the inn's formal name, means "Heihachi Teahouse-at-the-Foot-of-the-Mountains." Located on what was once the only road between Kyoto and the best fishing spots on the Japan Sea, it was the first stop for peddlers on their return trip to the capital; hence it received the freshest fish. When the railroad connecting Kyoto with the coast was built in the Meiji period, the peddlers no longer had to undertake the arduous hike. Heihachi-jaya began serving freshwater fish around the turn of the century, and now offers both ocean fish (*wakasa kaiseki*) and river fish (*seiryu kaiseki*) cuisine.

One of the unique features of Heihachi-jaya is the delightful *kamaburo*, an old-fashioned, Japanese-style clay sauna, heated from below the floor by pine wood gathered from the nearby forest. The *kamaburo* originated just north of here in Yase, several centuries ago, as a means of curing the battle scars of a young emperor. The "battle scars" of modern sightseeing can also be cured in the comfortable temperatures of the *kamaburo*, particularly when taken in combination with a fine meal. To enjoy the full beauty of an evening in northern Kyoto, have a relaxing sauna and bath, don a cotton

yukata robe, and stroll back through the garden to a private room overlooking the Takano River and a *kaiseki* meal. The *sansai*, or mountain greens, fresh grilled fish, and barley rice for which Heihachi-jaya is famous taste even better after the soothing sauna.

Though most of the original guest rooms were washed away during a terrible flood in 1789, the kitchen facing the highway was saved, and the original stone floors and giant rafters are just as they were in the Edo period. Peek inside as you pass by for a glimpse of the *daidokoro*, or kitchen, the heart of a traditional Japanese restaurant, where *sashimi* is sliced, and rice boiled, in the same way they have been for generations.

The amenities of sauna and private room are available not only to overnight guests at the inn, but also to those who come for the restaurant. If private rooms are not available, the spacious central dining room, which also overlooks the Takano River and the garden, is a quiet haven away from the noise and confusion of midtown. Heihachi-jaya offers fine food, a relaxing sauna, lush gardens, and a place to take off your shoes, unwind, and stay awhile.

HIIRAGI-YA

inn (ryokan)

Somehow, Hiiragi-ya still has the ambience of an inn catering to samurai. Something in the scale and aesthetics of the room—the black-lacquered trim of an alcove, the ornate gilded detail on a painted screen—join to suggest the luxury and privilege that belonged exclusively to the upper classes in Edo-period Japan.

Indeed, the samurai were among Hiiragi-ya's most frequent guests in the mid-nineteenth century. The inn was founded in 1861 by a man named Teijiro, a renowned metalsmith whose sword guards (*tsuba*) were sought after by the samurai. Teijiro's father, Shogoro, had left his hometown on the Japan Sea to establish a trading post in Kyoto. There he set up a boardinghouse for his porters, as well as for others who came to the capital in search of work. He named the inn after Hiiragi-jinja, his favorite shrine, which stands within the grounds of Shimogamo Shrine, just north of the fork in the Kamogawa River. "*Hiiragi*" also means "holly,"

and the holly leaf became the inn's logo.

After Shogoro's death in 1853, his son Teijiro the metalsmith was urged by his samurai friends to open an inn to accommodate the lords and their retainers from the provinces on their frequent trips to the capital. The decade that led up to the revolt that ousted the shogunate and reinstated the emperor as ruler of Japan was a time of political unrest in Kyoto. Daimyo, the rulers of the provinces, converged on the city, prepared to fight for one side or the other. Hiiragi-ya, in those days, was undoubtedly the scene of many a midnight intrigue session between samurai determined to champion their cause. Like most diplomatic Kyoto families, the present proprietress refrains from saying which side her samurai guests were on—possibly, we are led to suspect, both.

At various times in the inn's 125-year history, noted politicians and ministers of state, celebrities (including Charlie Chaplin), and famous writers

such as Yukio Mishima and Yasunari Kawabata have been guests at Hiiragi-ya. In one room you may sit at the same desk from which Mishima gazed out over the beautiful gardens with pen in hand. More extravagant in its tastes than its reserved neighbor, Tawara-ya, whose subdued decor calls to mind the philosophy of the tea ceremony, Hiiragi-ya has the luxurious sense of elegance associated with the old ruling class.

The exterior of Hiiragi-ya, whose long clay walls run all the way to the corner of Oike-dori, has the *komayose* wooden hitching post used in the days when samurai arrived in a flourish on horse-back. Each room has a private cedar *o-furo* bath, although, as is customary, the inn also has a central family-size bath, this one with large Meiji-period stained-glass windows.

A unique "modern" feature at Hiiragi-ya is the lacquered, push-button automatic control box that dims lights, opens and closes curtains, and calls the maid—an exotic-looking device invented by the former proprietor long before the push-button phone or the computer arrived in Japan. Hiiragi-ya, with its samurai flair and turn-of-the-century charm, is among the most beloved inns in Kyoto.

俵屋

TAWARA-YA

inn (ryokan)

"I would call back this world of shadows we are losing... I would have the eaves deep and the walls dark... I would strip away the useless decoration... I do not ask that this be done everywhere, but perhaps we may be allowed at least one mansion where we can turn off the electric lights and see what it is like without them."

The nostalgia that novelist Jun'ichiro Tanizaki felt for the shadowy beauty once so characteristic of the Japanese house is understandable when you see how rapidly modernization has changed the face of Kyoto. Even in the so-called traditional Japanese inns, it is not unusual to find a coin-operated TV set in the *tokonoma* alcove, formerly a place of honor in a Japanese room in which only a classic hanging scroll and a simple flower arrangement would be placed. Yet there is a place in Kyoto where the beauty of the play of light and shadow is still cherished. Tawara-ya is such a place—so precious that reservations are taken a year in advance for a night in Kyoto's quintessential inn.

At one time in Japanese history there were no inns in Kyoto. Emperors stayed in villas, visiting noblemen were accommodated by the Imperial Court, feudal lords made camp wherever they chose, pilgrims were put up at temples, craftsmen were too busy, city commoners couldn't afford it, and farmers were forbidden to travel at all. Only the merchants had reason (and permission) to roam the countryside peddling their wares. Fortunately for travelers in the twentieth century, a few of them tired of a life on the road and settled down in Kyoto, opening their homes to others like themselves who trod the long miles from country villages bearing heavy loads of rice to feed the imperial city.

Wasuke Okazaki, a textile merchant from a village called Tawara, was such a man. Nearly three hundred years ago, he sent his son to establish a post in Kyoto from which he could conduct business and provide lodging for his own employees and, eventually, for others whose lot it was to be on the road.

Gradually Tawara-ya gained a reputation for excellence. Since the turn of the century the inn has been host to the noble and the famous from all over the world. Members of the imperial family have stayed there, as did Hirobumi Ito, the first prime minister of Japan. The guest book bears

the names of Rothschilds and Rockefellers—even of Marlon Brando.

The present owner, Toshi (Okazaki) Sato, maintains a classic Japanese inn with all the traditional beauty but without the usual inconveniences: no need to share the bath, no bone-chilling mornings without proper heat, no sweltering afternoons with droning electric fans.

It is possible to lose yourself down the long, twisting corridors of Tawara-ya, where each turn reveals another intimate scene: a folding screen adorned with a mountain scene in the Zen style of brush painting, an arrangement of wildflowers in a natural salt-glazed ceramic vase, a stone water basin into which cold, clear water drips slowly from a bamboo spout. Nowhere but here do corridors flicker with the soft candlelight of a dozen lacquered antique lamps.

Every room is different. Each is furnished simply but elegantly with fine antiques that have been in the Okazaki family for generations—lacquered tables, brocade armrests, intricately woven bamboo basketry. Every room has a private bath done in ceramic tiles from a local kiln, and cedar baths whose fragrance scents the air like a mountain breeze.

With all this to speak for it, Sato-san maintains that the key to the Tawara-ya's success is simply the service. There are only nineteen rooms, so each guest receives fastidious personal care, from the friendly old gentleman who takes your shoes at the door to the charming lady in kimono who welcomes you to your room with a hot hand towel and a fresh pot of tea. Even the elderly gardener bows as you pass the stand of new bamboo where he is busily snipping off a leaf that has outlived its time.

Saul Bellow summed up the sentiments of all the guests who've spent a peaceful night at Tawara-ya: "I found here what I had hoped to find in Japan—the human scale, tranquility, and beauty." How Tanizaki would have envied his good fortune.

KINMATA
inn (ryokan), restaurant

No gambling.
No prostitution.
No mahjong.
No credit.
No noisy parties …

So begins the long list of house rules that has hung in the hallway at Kinmata since the nineteenth century. No arbitrary mandate from the innkeeper, these were the rules of the day for all Japanese inns (*ryokan*) under the Tokugawa shogunate, whose rigid reign proscribed the daily life of citizens down to the finest detail.

Seven generations later, Haruji Ukai, the young innkeeper at Kinmata, still insists on peace and quiet in his nearly two-hundred-year-old inn. Though the inn is located in the very heart of the downtown area, its interior recesses are surprisingly removed from the noise of the city.

In 1801, the year Kinmata opened for business, the most frequent guests were traveling salesmen bringing herbal medicines to Kyoto from Omi and Shiga near Lake Biwa to the east. A few old medicine peddlers' *kanban*, or signboards, are kept in the entryway as mementos of the inn's first customers.

The meals at the family-run Kinmata are planned and prepared by the innkeeper himself, who was apprenticed as a boy with a fishmonger in the Nishiki street market just half a block away. Nishiki Koji is where the most famous of Kyoto's restaurateurs shop for the ingredients of their elegant *kaiseki*

KIKAKU-TEI

inn (ryokan), restaurant

Yase is a small rural town that clings to the foot of Mt. Hiei in the northeastern corner of Kyoto like a shy child clutching her mother's apron strings. The single, narrow road that leads to Yase and Ohara beyond was once the only trade route between the ancient capital and the Japan Sea. The old road through the mountain pass was arduous and exhausting.

For centuries Yase has been known as a place to relax, to recover, to enjoy at the end of a long journey. The name Yase literally means "eight springs," for here a number of small streams flow into the Takano River as it makes its way to the Kamogawa River in the heart of Kyoto. But local legends tell of a different origin to the village's name. Once in the seventh century after the death of the emperor Tenji, the armies of the emperor's illegitimate son fought his brother for control of the throne. The brother (later known as Emperor Tenmu) won, but not without suffering a near-fatal arrow wound in the back. The battle took place at Omi on the other side of the mountain near Lake Biwa, and his men carried their wounded lord over the mountains to safety in a tiny village by a river and stayed with him until he recovered. The villagers say what pulled him through was the *kamaburo*, an oven-like steambath in which he could lie flat on his stomach while his arrow wound healed. The village became known thereafter as Yase, or "arrow-in-the-back," when written with characters different from those used today.

Kikaku-tei is a *kamaburo* inn, hidden at the edge of the forest beside the Takanogawa river in Yase. It was once the elegant villa of Hiroshi Tanaka, the industrial magnate who founded the famous Miyako Hotel in Kyoto. Among other things, he owned Kyoto's first electric power company and established the Keifuku train line that runs from Demachi (where the Takano and Kamogawa rivers meet in Kyoto) to Kurama (in the mountains north of the city) and on to Yase, just across the river from Kikaku-tei.

The Keifuku train has, thankfully, never really been modernized. You sit on velvet covered seats as the old one-car electric train rumbles up out of the

cuisine. His early training and present proximity give Ukai-san an inside lead on the finest of the day's catch, and the seafood meals prepared at Kinmata have become as popular as the traditional beauty of the inn itself. *Kaiseki*-style formal meals are served either in the newly remodeled front dining room or, with advance reservations, in one of the original private rooms of the inn.

In the inn itself, Ukai-san has kept the original furnishings and decor of the old-style *ryokan*. Fine lacquered *andon* lanterns and mirrored dressing stands (*kyodai*), curved cedar handrails, and two bamboo-fenced interior gardens contribute to the atmosphere of traditional Japanese hospitality. Kinmata has only nine rooms in all and welcomes anyone who appreciates the intimate atmosphere and gracious amenities of an old-style Japanese inn (and respects the innkeeper's request for peace and quiet).

The large communal bath (*o-furo*) downstairs was recently redone in solid *hinoki* (cypress wood) with its own tiny window-box garden; it offers the classical Japanese "soak" that is said to relieve all the tension and stress a medicine peddler—or a modern traveler—can accumulate in a hectic day.

city to Yase at the end of the short line. It takes about twenty minutes. Climbing down from the platform you walk a few meters to a creaky old footbridge that (hopefully) takes you across the Takano River to a dirt path leading to the right, past a small waterfall and on to the inn. Stone walls surround the former villa and a single tile-roofed gateway leads enticingly up the stone steps and out of the real world. Giant maple trees hide the secluded inn from view as you begin to climb the mossy steps.

The rooms in the north wing are smaller and on more of a personal scale than the luxurious main rooms in the south wing. At the end of the corridor in the north wing is a beautifully designed tearoom.

The south wing (originally the main house) is separated by a long corridor leading across more garden so that every room has a sweeping view.

Kikaku-tei was turned into a *ryokan* after the owners passed away. The old villa seems a bit disgruntled at having been turned into an inn. Not as polished perhaps as some of its prima donna counterparts in mid-town, Kikaku-tei speaks with the voice of an era in Japanese history, not so very long ago, when the very wealthy few lived a life of sequestered elegance and luxury.

The *kamaburo* at Kikaku-tei can be used anytime, before or after dinner and again in the morning if the guest so chooses. Not as hot as a Swedish sauna, the round clay oven-shaped *kamaburo* is the original Japanese way to unwind and heal your wounds, be they sore feet or overtaxed senses.

The meals at Kikaku-tei feature freshwater fish in season, whether as a part of a full-course *kaiseki* meal, or in *kamayaki*, the one-pot specialty of the house—a bountiful feast of seafood, mushrooms, and vegetables simmered in a delicious broth at your table. (*Kamaburo* privileges are also available to guests who come only for dinner, but reservations are required.)

• C H R O N O L O G Y •

NARA
710–94

HEIAN
794–1185

KAMAKURA
1185–1333

MUROMACHI
1333–1568

MOMOYAMA
1568–1600

EDO
1600–1868

MEIJI
1868–1912

TAISHO
1912–26

SHOWA
1926–1989

HEISEI
1989 to present

HISTORY

The folk that have been attracted thither and the poets do all with one voice acclaim this Heian-kyo, the capital of peace and tranquility.

> Emperor Kanmu.
>
> 794, eleventh month, eighth day

In 1994, the city of Kyoto celebrated the twelve-hundredth anniversary of the founding of Emperor Kanmu's new capital in a quiet valley in Central Japan. Shunning the political entanglements that beset the Imperial Court in Nara, he made a fresh start here in October 794.

Little did he know that the name he bestowed on his city—Heian-Kyo, "capital of peace and tranquility" —would one day become a classic irony. For over a thousand years, Kyoto, as it is now known, was the scene of endless wars and political strife, and the victim of more than its share of devastating natural disasters. It was, indeed, the birthplace of one of the most refined and sophisticated cultures on earth; yet it was far from the peaceful citadel Kanmu had envisioned.

Kanmu chose the site for a number of reasons: pronounced "spiritually correct" by court geomancers, it was surrounded on three sides by mountains that made it a natural fortress. It had an endless, if capricious, supply of water from the Kamogawa river that divides it in two. It was also home to 130,000 members of the Hata clan, descendants of Chinese immigrants, who could teach his craftsmen how to weave—and lend him the money to build his palace.

Kanmu's dream was to create an imperial city that would rival Chang-an, the glorious capital of Tang-dynasty China. His comprehensive plan for the layout of the city patterned the valley floor with a permanent grid of streets, that divided the entire area into precise rectangular blocks, as in the Chinese model he sought to outdo.

During the 390 years of relative calm now known as the Heian period, Kanmu's descendants led a life of luxury and elegance within the palace walls, in an atmosphere of isolated splendor that rivaled the excesses of Versailles. It was a Golden Age that developed a refined literary and artistic tradition whose achievements have yet to be rivaled. But the exquisite life of the court also resulted in a weakening of imperial determination to deal with the mundane business of governing the land, leaving the powerful local clans to fight over it for several centuries to come. It was the Fujiwara clan who, assuming the role of regents by marrying into the imperial family, dominated this first age of scrambled Kyoto politics.

The presence of the emperor and his ambitious entourage made Kyoto a bustling hub of craftsmanship, as well as the center of the political scene. Artisans skilled in sophisticated techniques imported from China during the previous century were called to the new capital to provide the accoutrements and luxuries required to maintain the extravagant lifestyle of the Imperial Court. Merchants came flocking in to supply the materials, foods, and commodities necessary to build and support a growing city. Two marketplaces were established, in the southeast and southwest of the city, where they could exchange their wares. These were lively places where people of all ranks, from noblemen to peasants, walked about examining the latest products and wares. The Eastern Market, where

Kyoto Station now stands, flourished, but the Western Market died out, establishing the eastern half as the city center as early as the tenth century.

By the twelfth century, however, it had become obvious that the townspeople would have to band together in order to defend themselves against an endless stream of military and natural disasters. Neighborhoods grouped themselves into tightly knit communities around shrines and temples. Some of them built moatlike ditches around their neighborhoods for protection or for flood control, crop irrigation, and defense against the frequent fires that plagued a city built entirely of wood and thatch.

It was during this era of natural and manmade disaster that Kamo no Chomei, the hermit poet, sat alone in his hut on a mountainside near Ohara, bemoaning the fate of the city he loved:

> The flow of the river is ceaseless, but the water is never the same. In the still pools the shifting foam gathers and is gone, never staying for a moment. Even

mourned the devastating price the people of Kyoto paid for the honor of inhabiting the ancient capital. And perhaps he realized that change was the only constant upon which the populace could depend.

The military government established by the Minamoto clan when the Fujiwara family finally went into decline was so busy holding its own that it had neither the time, inclination, nor means to help the commoners rebuild their row houses after every battle, fire, or flood. By the time Minamoto no Yoritomo had himself proclaimed shogun in 1192, a large portion of the city had been devastated, and the starving townspeople were left to their own devices when he moved his headquarters to Kamakura in the east.

The ability of the merchants and craftsmen to band together in mini-townships enabled them to undertake reconstruction on their own. The crisscross pattern of the city streets provided manageable blocks in which groups of merchants and craftsmen worked together to rebuild their homes and shops. The unity

so is man and his habitation. In the stately ways of our shining Capital the dwellings of high and low raise their roofs in rivalry as in the beginning, but few indeed there are that have stood for generations. This year falling into decay and the next built up again— how often do the mansions of one age turn into the cottages of the next.... Like the dew on the morning glory are man and his house—who knows which will survive the other?

He watched as torrents of political turmoil swept away the elegance and refinement of what would later be called the "Golden Age" of Japanese history. He

and self-determination that evolved in these neighborhoods at the beginning of the twelfth century was to help them survive the rise and fall of a succession of military leaders over the next four hundred years.

The arrival of Zen from China at the end of the twelfth century was to have a great impact on Japanese culture. This austere sect of Buddhism, with its emphasis on training of body and mind, was attractive to the shogun and his samurai; the strength and discipline that it encouraged was a welcome change from the weak life of luxury that they saw as a primary factor in the decline of both emperor and regents. The great Zen temples that were built in the following century served as centers of culture in Kyoto throughout the age of political instability to come. Zen priests encouraged continued contact with China, offering Kyoto merchants and craftsmen the opportunity to begin a prosperous trade network that gave them the economic strength, not only to survive, but to flourish when other sectors of society collapsed. They began to form guilds called *za*, which were under the protection of the shrines and temples on whose grounds they held regular markets in return for the payment of special taxes.

Yet another coup in the early fourteenth century brought the Ashikaga shogunate to power, reestablishing Kyoto as the center of political power. The 235 years of Ashikaga reign were characterized by unparalleled cultural development, contrasting with equally unmatched political and social disaster. The Ashikaga shoguns, firm followers of Zen, were great patrons of the arts. In the Muromachi period, named for the palace they built near the emperor's quarters in Kyoto, ink

the Kamogawa river flooded, washing away two major bridges. In 1444, when merchants took over Kitano Shrine in an appeal for just government, shogunate forces slashed their way in, forced the merchants to commit mass suicide, and proceeded to set fire to the shrine, which burned to the ground. In the decade before Yoshimasa's birth, warrior-priests of the Enryaku-ji temple on Mt. Hiei stormed down the mountainside on a number of occasions, wielding the feared portable shrine (said to possess the power of life and death) to make demands on the Imperial Court. The year 1447 brought severe earthquakes and floods, and 1449, the year Yoshimasa was born, marked the beginning of a terrible plague that took the lives of a thousand citizens a day. By the time Yoshimasa was ten years old, a massive famine had left great funerary mounds all over the besieged capital city.

Depressed—to say the least—by the condition of the kingdom he had inherited, Yoshimasa chose to abandon his duties as shogun at the age of thirty-five,

painting, calligraphy, and tea ceremony all flourished. The third Ashikaga shogun, Yoshimitsu, built the magnificent Kinkaku-ji, the Gold Pavilion, in the northwest of Kyoto in 1397.

But by the middle of the fifteenth century, Kyoto was again the scene of a power struggle between the daimyo from the provinces who, craving a taste of the famed luxury at court, flocked to the capital city.

The realm inherited by Ashikaga Yoshimasa, grandson of Yoshimitsu, was in a state of total chaos. It was as if the mid-fifteenth century had been singled out for retribution by a legion of angry gods. In 1442

spending the rest of his years at Ginkaku-ji, the Silver Pavilion, his equally exquisite if less glamorous version of his grandfather's villa on the opposite side of the city. The villa faced the Higashiyama Hills, and the whole culture that flourished under Yoshimasa's patronage was named after them—*Higashiyama Bunka*, or the "Culture of the Eastern Hills."

On the brighter side for the city's craftsmen and merchants, the Muromachi period also saw the development of the tea ceremony, whose popularity stimulated in turn the production of ceramic bowls and flower vases, bamboo basketry and utensils, cast-metal teakettles, and lacquer ware. It also created a need for skilled carpenters and gardeners capable of building and caring for tearooms and landscape gardens, and established an aesthetic norm for ordinary Japanese architecture.

The succession dispute touched off by Yoshimasa's early retirement led to the Onin War (1467–77), a disastrous ten-year conflict that leveled the city, ruining both contending parties, and yet ironically failing to settle the original dispute. Hardly a building was left standing. After the war, the merchant townships set about rebuilding their city with little or no help from either the shogunate or the noblemen,

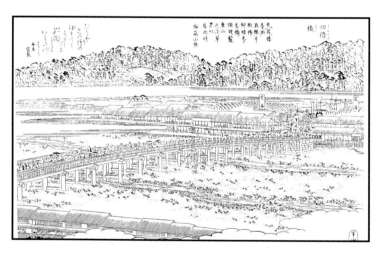

who were either disinterested in the fate of the peasants or in nearly as desperate shape themselves. A recorded eighty-two thousand citizens died of starvation in 1480. Even the Imperial Court fell into such a state of poverty that the emperor himself had to resort to the sale of calligraphy to survive.

The merchants, however, who by now had acquired the acumen to take advantage of the constantly shifting political winds, had accumulated the wealth necessary to put the city back on its feet by providing food and supplies to both sides of a succession of competing armies. For the talent of hiding their true sympathies, Kyoto merchants earned a reputation for being "two-faced"—a trait they are still accused of from time to time today.

By the middle of the sixteenth century, the winds of war had once again begun to blow the wrong way. When St. Francis Xavier arrived in Kyoto in 1551, he

was the first Western traveler to see the ancient city—or what was left of it. He wrote:

"Today much of Kyoto lies in ruins because of the wars; many people have told us that it once had eighteen thousand houses, and it seems to me that this must have been true, to judge from the very large size of the city."

When the Ashikaga shogunate fell, the rough-and-tumble Oda Nobunaga was there to grab power. Although he did much to unify the country that had for so long been at the mercy of warring factions, he did not endear himself to the people of Kyoto. He burned down over four hundred temples at Enryaku-ji on Mt. Hiei, Kyoto's sacred mountain, because of the threat its powerful priests presented to his own regime. He then proceeded to wipe out a large portion of the northeastern sector of the city—not yet well organized into communities—for inability to pay his exorbitant taxes.

It was Toyotomi Hideyoshi, Nobunaga's successor, who did the most to rebuild Kyoto. During this period at the end of the sixteenth century, the merchants and craftsmen came to his aid by helping with the reconstruction of the many temples that had been destroyed during the Onin War. Hideyoshi had dreams of restoring the city to a higher level of grandeur than even Kanmu himself could have imagined. In 1591, he ordered construction of a great wall that would surround the entire city; today, only a few crumbling mementos have survived the centuries. Besides rebuilding temples and shrines, Hideyoshi enlisted the aid of Kyoto merchants and craftsmen in the construction of a magnificent pleasure palace, Juraku-dai, which he built on the ruins of the imperial palace itself.

It was during this period that groups of townspeople began to organize the neighborhood communities called machi (or cho), which undertook much of the reconstruction on their own. With the rebuilding of the city, the merchant class eventually became so prosperous that it started to create its own separate world of art and culture. This "floating world" typically depicted in woodblock prints was a realm of decadence and often excess, but of a luxury that existed for the first time for the common people.

Surrounded now by substantial wealth, the townspeople were in a position to begin refining their daily lives. Inspired by the aesthetics of the tea ceremony, formerly the preserve of the upper classes, the merchants employed master carpenters (hitherto only available to the samurai warriors and nobility) to create a living environment embodying all that was finest in contemporary Kyoto society: the spiritual qualities of the Zen priesthood, the refined tastes of the nobility, the austere restraint of the warriors, the skill of the finest craftsmen, the simplicity of peasants, and the sense of unflagging practicality that had brought the prospering merchant class this far.

Although the death of Hideyoshi and the rise of Tokugawa Ieyasu took the seat of government east to Edo (now Tokyo) in 1603, this left Kyoto's merchants and craftsmen free to spend the next two hundred years developing the arts and crafts for which the city is famous. By imitating the trappings of the life of upper-class samurai—who, with no wars left to wage, were practically out of work—the merchants aspired to raise their lowly social status. So they patronized the arts—pottery, textiles, lacquering, paper-making, painting, gardening, architecture....

By the middle of the Edo period, the shogunate, feeling threatened by the merchants' rise in power, began legislating every detail of the latter's lives, right down to the size of the dolls their children were allowed to own. Not only did the shogunate put an end to almost all traffic with foreign countries in 1639, but it also issued a long list of restrictions intended to keep the merchants in their place. There were to be no more elaborate hair combs, parasols, or silk kimonos, and no "selling of peculiar things to hit the public fancy." The rules of conduct issued for the peasants were even more restrictive: they were to get up early, were not to buy saké or tea, were not to smoke, and were to divorce a wife who took too much tea or wasted time on casual excursions.

In spite of these rigid codes, it was, by the middle of the eighteenth century, too late for the shogunate to control the merchants any longer; they were well on their way to becoming the economic wizards that run the country today. The townhouses, *machiya*, that they lived in grew bigger—sometimes almost overnight—during the welter of rebuilding after every fire that plagued the tinderbox city. With each reconstruction, they extended their property lines further into the streets, making it a real art for cars today to navigate between phone poles planted right on the shoulder and children on bicycles with no other place to play. The servants and employees of the merchants were relegated to humble dwellings off the main boulevards, in narrow alleys some of which still exist. The merchants owned the land on which their workers lived, and at

the same time relied upon them to work in their shops and make the products they sold, thus establishing a pattern of mutual dependence which to some extent has survived to the present day within the old neighborhoods of Kyoto.

The shops of Kyoto and their keepers continued to flourish until one bone-chilling morning late in the winter of 1788. A wind suddenly blew in from the east with a force unheard of in Kyoto—a city which, because it lies in a basin, is usually thankful for the slightest breeze to break the stillness of its captive air—bowling over street stalls, peddlers, even horses. Somewhere along the west bank of the Kamogawa river, a fire broke out in a money changer's shop that had given way before the hurricane gusts. By dawn the next day the entire city was in flames; three days later 183,000 homes, 909 temples, and 37 shrines had been reduced to ash. Virtually no wooden structure in the city center remains that pre-dates the monstrous Tenmei Fire. Again the townspeople had a city to rebuild.

The end of the eighteenth century was a difficult time not only for the citizens of Kyoto, but for the entire nation as well. The shogunate was in disastrous economic straits, having borrowed funds to finance the extravagant tastes of the growing population of non-productive samurai. The samurai themselves had begun to borrow money from the merchants, and fell further and further into debt.

A series of major famines occurred at the end of the eighteenth and in the early nineteenth century. Over a million peasants died of starvation during the great famine of 1780–86. The Tokugawa shogunate was ineffectual, despite new laws calling for a return to austerity among the samurai, who by now were accustomed to an indolent life of luxury. A succession of weak Tokugawa shoguns noted only for their administrative incompetence ensured the decline of the shogunate's power throughout the land. With the aid of dissatisfied daimyo, an impoverished and restless populace began plotting the overthrow of the shogunate and the restoration of the emperor as ruler of Japan.

When Commodore Perry's ships sailed into port on July 8, 1853, the country was ready for change. His demands for the opening of trade with the United States ended over two hundred years of self-enforced isolation. Renewed commerce with the West was to have a major impact on Japanese culture from then on. Intrigued by the guns and machinery the foreigners brought with them, the Japanese sought to acquire many of the "advanced" accoutrements of Western life.

For Kyoto, still the home of the emperor, this era of change and confusion meant that it would once again be the site of a major battle. Unrest in the provinces brought vassals to Kyoto to "save the emperor" from the hands of a shogun struggling to maintain control. Plotters with hopes of restoring the emperor to power held clandestine meetings at now-famous inns; deep gashes in the beams and corner posts of some of these attest to their eagerness to try out their swords. One skirmish led to a fire in the Kyoto hideout of a provincial clan leader, again leaving much of the city devastated in 1864. Within four short years, however, the people of Kyoto had once again rebuilt the entire city.

Lacking the support of the majority of the daimyo, the last shogun surrendered power in 1868, and the court of the Emperor Meiji moved to Edo in the same year, renaming the city Tokyo, the "Eastern Capital."

The emperor's departure broke the hearts of the people of Kyoto. Their civic pride was bound to a centuries-old image of Kyoto as the "Imperial City," and an air of depression hung over the valley for a number of years, leading to a great decline in production of the local arts and crafts in the years that followed.

But 1894 marked the eleven-hundredth anniversary of Kyoto, which the people commemorated by building the Heian shrine, a replica of the original Imperial Palace. A creative governor ordered the construction of a waterway that linked the city to Lake Biwa in the east, making possible the completion of an electric power plant and the installation of Japan's first electric street cars. A measure of civic pride was restored to the determined populace.

The period that followed was a time of welcome peace for the people of Kyoto. Craftsmen continued to hone the skills for which they had become world famous. The caste system proscribed by Tokugawa was finally abolished, leaving citizens of all classes freer than ever before to pursue the livelihood of their choice. A flurry of new shops opened around the turn of the century.

World War II was the next—and hopefully the last—major catastrophe to disrupt the lives of the citizens of Kyoto. Fortunately, the Americans opted to save the ancient capital city, and it was not destroyed in firebombings such as leveled Tokyo and Osaka. Then Secretary of War Henry Stimson pleaded that the city be saved out of respect for its historical and cultural importance, and Kyoto was removed from the top of the list of cities targeted for the atomic bomb.

Uncertainty, however, caused city fathers to order the widening of Kyoto's most important thoroughfares to act as possible firebreaks if such a tragedy should occur. This resulted in the loss of over eighteen thousand fine old shops and houses. Furthermore, the large number of merchants and craftsmen enlisted by the Imperial Army and killed in the war caused a drastic decline in the number of shops left in Kyoto when Japan surrendered in 1945. After the war, materials were scarce and difficult to obtain, forcing many craftsmen to seek other employment. Before World War II there were over a hundred bucket makers in Kyoto; today they can be counted on one hand.

The trend toward Americanization after the war also left its mark. Young people began to prefer American-style products, mass-produced in five shades of plastic, to the laboriously handmade breakables made by their grandfathers. Fast foods, fast cars, and high-rise buildings represent the latest hazards to life in Kyoto. The old shops that remain must contend with these latest threats to their existence—more insidious foes than fire or famine. They must either find ways to adjust to changing Japanese tastes and make their products fit twentieth-century life, or fade away.

Hopefully, the strength of will and stubborn determination the people of Kyoto have shown over the past eleven centuries will help them through this most recent difficulty, too. Perhaps they will be able to resist the pressure of economic forces that seek to redevelop the city center, forcing out the old shops and their tenants, changing forever the historical character and sense of community that has enabled its citizens to survive this long. Theirs has been a legacy of change... a history of elegance and disaster...constantly flowing, never the same.

Raku-chu, Raku-gai — Kyoto's Quarters

Even before the Emperor Kanmu made it the site of his imperial city in 794, the Hata and Kamo clans had established a village in this valley called Uda, and built the shrines—Kamigamo, Shimogamo, Matsuo, Fushimi Inari—that are still popular today. *Miyako*, which simply means capital, was the colloquial expression for Kyoto. *Miyako e agaru* meant to "go up to the capital." Since the capital is now Tokyo, however, the proper use of *agaru* (go up) and *sagaru* (go down) is now a bone of contention between residents of the two proud cities.

The prefix *raku* (the Japanese pronunciation of the Chinese character meaning capital city) came into use in the Heian period primarily as a means of defining the boundaries of the capital city. Surrounded at one time by a huge wall, everything inside the city was

called Raku-chu; everything outside was Raku-gai. Folding screen paintings called *Raku-chu-Raku-gai-zu Byobu* were popular during the Edo period, illustrating the lives of the common people in maplike, bird's eye views of the city streets.

As the city grew, it became necessary to refer to specific regions outside the city proper, so the four directions were added: Raku-hoku, north of the capital; Raku-to, east; Raku-nan, south; and Raku-sei, west.

The exact borders of each district were never precisely defined, and in the Meiji period, in the late nineteenth century, a more complicated division of ward precincts was made by the government. The traditional names, however, persist; Raku-chu, Raku-hoku, Raku-to, Raku-nan, and Raku-sei are now used whenever there is a desire to define the character, both culturally and physically—the historical and aesthetic personality, as it were—that has evolved in each area over the centuries.

The scholarly priest of Raku-to; the honest farmer of Raku-hoku; the melancholy ladies of Raku-sei; the down-to-earth laborer of Raku-nan; the wily merchant of Raku-chu—each is a formidable character, each a pleasure to get to know.

Raku-chu, Central Kyoto

As the heart of the old capital city, Raku-chu is still the busiest, most densely populated area in Kyoto. Most of the shops, both old and new, for which the city is famous are here in a broad area that runs from Kita-oji in the north to just below Kyoto Station in the south, and from Nishi-oji in the west to the Kamogawa River in the east. It corresponds roughly to the district which the Emperor Kanmu first branded with a grid pattern of streets in 794, though by the eleventh century the center of the city had shifted to the east of the area, where it remains today.

The area around the Imperial Palace, the focal point of both politics and commerce, was inhabited by wealthy men of power, and today is home to merchants and craftsmen whose ancestors were Purveyors to the Imperial Household before the capital was transferred to what is now Tokyo in 1868. Nijo Castle, built by Tokugawa Ieyasu in the seventeenth century, is in Raku-chu.

The Nishijin weaving district is located in the northwestern part of Raku-chu. Yuzen dyeing is done in workshops to the west and southwest of the Imperial Palace. Kimono merchants line Muromachi-dori in the area called Yamaboko-cho, where the floats for Gion Matsuri are kept—the heart of Raku-chu. Downtown, near Kawaramachi-Shijo, you'll find Pontocho, the geisha quarter; Nishiki, the city's oldest market street; and Teramachi, once a temple district and now an area of booksellers, antique dealers, and shops selling utensils for the tea ceremony.

Just north of Kyoto Station are the two great temples of the Pure Land Sect of Buddhism, Nishi- and Higashi-Hongan-ji. Between them stretches a neighborhood of shops that make religious articles— candles, incense, prayer beads, and Buddhist altars.

Raku-chu—bustling, vibrant, and eclectic—with its contrast (and sometimes conflict) between old and new, is the heart of Kyoto and the home of many of its finest traditional shops.

Raku-to, Eastern Kyoto

The foothills of Higashiyama (the "Eastern Mountains") represent an area of elegance and distinction stretching from Ginkaku-ji, the Silver Pavilion, in the north, all the way to Sanjusangen-do, the Hall of a-Thousand-and-One Kannon, in the south Kiyomizu-dera, the grande dame of Kyoto temples, has drawn pilgrims to Raku-to since the Heian period. The cobbled paths that lead up to it are lined with ceramics shops, some of which date from the Edo period, when the area was the main pottery district in Kyoto, producing the delicately painted ware known as Kiyomizu-yaki. The sixty-seven-ton bronze bell of Chion-in, of the popular Jodo Sect of Buddhism, has tolled the arrival of every New Year in Kyoto since the seventh century, and the Silver Pavilion, where the

shogun Ashikaga Yoshimasa held his elegant tea ceremonies, still stands as a symbol of the heights of culture attained in Raku-to four hundred years ago. The Higashiyama area was associated with a whole culture including the tea ceremony and a variety of other refined arts and crafts—flower arrangement, ink painting, ceramics, and garden design, to name but a few.

Raku-to has always been the home of temples, great and small, to which emperors fled whenever the palace down in the center of Kyoto was threatened by fire or war. Shoguns and retired emperors built their villas here, and it was at temples such as Nanzen-ji in the center of Raku-to that Zen became the influential force in Japanese society it remains today. Black-robed monks, begging bowls in hand, can even now be heard at dawn chanting for alms in the neighborhoods around this still-vital Zen center.

At the turn of the century, the lovely path that follows an old canal from the foot of Ginkaku-ji southward was discovered by the scholars of what was then the Imperial University of Kyoto. Known as the "Philosophers' Walk," this path beneath cherry blossoms in spring and maple leaves in fall is as popular today

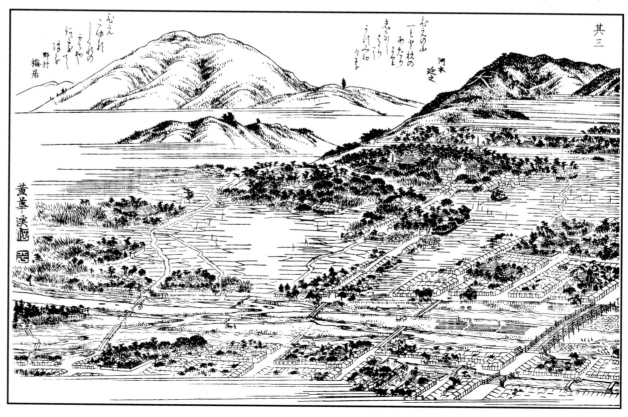

with young lovers as it once was with intellectuals.

In Okazaki Park, with its art museums, library, and zoo, stands Heian Shrine, a replica of the original Imperial Palace buildings that were lost to fire in the feudal ages, and its splendid stroll garden, both built at the turn of the century to celebrate Kyoto's eleven-hundredth anniversary as a city.

Kyoto's most famous geisha quarter, Gion, is in Raku-to. Here the streets are lined with old teahouses whence the sound of *shamisen* music still floats on warm summer nights. In the early evening young *maiko* apprentices in all their finery can be seen hurrying off to entertain guests with an evening of drink and dance. If you have but one day free to spend in Kyoto on your own, walk the paths at the foot of Higashiyama—whether it be philosophy or femininity that strikes your fancy.

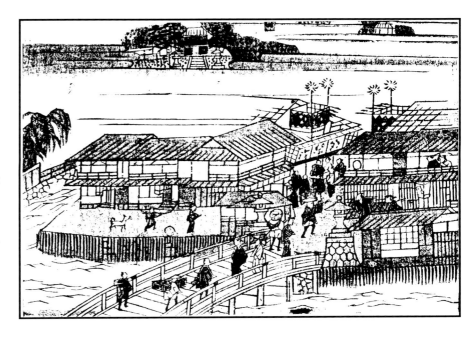

Raku-hoku, Northern Kyoto

Raku-hoku is about all the "country" Kyoto has left. Until recent years the area was famous for its vegetables and rice fields, but those days are largely a thing of the past. The northeast sector of Raku-hoku was once a district of flower growers and herbalists. Women in *monpe* trousers and white bandannas, a rare sight today, used to pull their heavy carts down from the fields to the palace to provide flowers for the emperor. They can still be seen occasionally in the geisha quarter, delivering their flowers to teahouses along the old canal.

Directly to the north are two famous shrines that existed even before the city was founded here in the eighth century—Shimogamo and Kamigamo. The latter, farther north than its partner, is surrounded by the old clay-walled estates of the families of Shinto priests who have tended to the shrine for over ten centuries. It is a pleasant place for a stroll to catch a glimpse of what remains of rural Kyoto. The old shops in this neighborhood are famous for old-fashioned country-style pickles made with vegetables grown in the few fields that remain.

Daitoku-ji, the oldest Zen temple in Kyoto, standing just north of Kita-oji (the approximate southern boundary of Raku-hoku), harbors some of the city's most exquisite Zen rock gardens. Associated with the famous schools of tea, the temple is also known among gourmets for its fine Zen vegetarian cuisine (*shojin-*

ryori), available both on the premises and outside its eastern gate.

Far to the north, nestled beside rivers in the mountain passes that lead to the Japan Sea, several small villages that can be reached within a few minutes by bus or train are popular among visitors and city dwellers who wish to escape for a day and spend a refreshing few hours in the Kitayama Mountains: Kibune, to visit the old shrine there and to dine, in summer, at a table built right over a clear mountain stream...Kurama, for a stroll through an old post town whose old shops and houses still retain the sense of a reststop for weary peddlers arriving in the capital city bearing goods for trade from the Japan Sea...Ohara, for a classic mountain village with small temples in which an exiled empress and a number of poets and hermits lived out their melancholy days in rural quiet...or Yase, now the site of an amusement park, but still the home of the thousand-year-old *kamaburo* steam baths that once healed a wounded emperor on his way home from battle. Shugakuin Imperial Villa, a serene reminder of a gracious rural past, is also located in Raku-hoku.

Raku-hoku, though it has recently become a popular residential area for merchants weary of sardine life in the crowded city, still has an air of country living—though the once-famous symphony of frogs in its rice fields has been reduced by now to a quiet sonata....

Raku-sei, Western Kyoto

Arashiyama...even the name evokes "autumn" in the minds of anyone who has ever visited this beautiful ravine in November. The steep mountain slopes, with their seasonal wardrobes of crimson and green, have been a favorite haunt of Japanese emperors for centuries. Togetsu-kyo, the bridge that spans the wide Oi River, marks the center of the area. While at a boating party here, the thirteenth-century emperor Kameoka, wrote the poem from which the bridge's name is derived:

Crossing the river—
like
the moon.

North from this romantic bridge, the fields and bamboo groves of Sagano, dotted with the thatched rooftops of a dozen small country temples, stretch past Tenryu-ji temple with its dragon ceiling, all the way to the *torii* gate which leads to Atago Shrine. Further

north are Ninna-ji, with its pair of snarling Nio figures guarding the gate; Ryoan-ji, with its world-famous rock garden; and Kinkaku-ji, the Gold Pavilion built by the shogun Ashikaga Yoshimitsu in the fourteenth century.

Raku-sei, renowned for its scenic beauty, was also a place of exile for court ladies who had fallen out of favor with their lords. The melancholy aura of small temples like Gio-ji, named after one such lady who shaved her head and lived out her years here in shame, have given Raku-sei a feeling of wistful romance that appeals to the young women who flock here every year.

In the early centuries of Kyoto's history, Raku-sei was abandoned as an uninhabitable lowland of swamps, in favor of the more favorably situated eastern sector. There are few old shops to visit along the way, compared with other parts of the city, but the quiet mountains, rivers, and fields, and the many small country temples, restaurants, and inns make this area the best in Kyoto for a leisurely stroll away from the noisy city.

Raku-nan, Southern Kyoto

Raku-nan, the only side of Kyoto unprotected by mountains, was thus the main transportation route to the old port of Sakai (now Osaka) on the Inland Sea to the south. Fragments of the highway used by samurai and peddlers in the Edo period still exist, as do post towns such as Fushimi. Fushimi Inari is the home of a shrine to the Rice Goddess which pre-dates the founding of Heian-kyo in 794; its festival every February still attracts thousands of merchants and businessmen who come to pray for a successful year. Fushimi Momoyama, formerly a castle town at the foot of Toyotomi Hideyoshi's great sixteenth-century fortress Fushimi-jo, is now one of the two biggest saké-producing towns in Japan, with thirty-seven different breweries within walking distance of each other, standing around a canal that was once a main thoroughfare for flatboats carrying goods back and forth from Kyoto to Sakai. It takes just fifteen minutes to reach Fushimi by train from Sanjo-Keihan Station, but that is enough to push Fushimi off the normal tourist path. If you are looking for a side of Kyoto that hasn't been tinted for the travel posters, Fushimi is the place to find it.

Raku-nan belongs to the common people. It has never had the frills and finery of areas in the north that were closer to the imperial palace. This is where "the people" lived—and still live. Industrial, straightforward, and real, it is a fine place to have a taste of what life is like away from the Famous Sites.

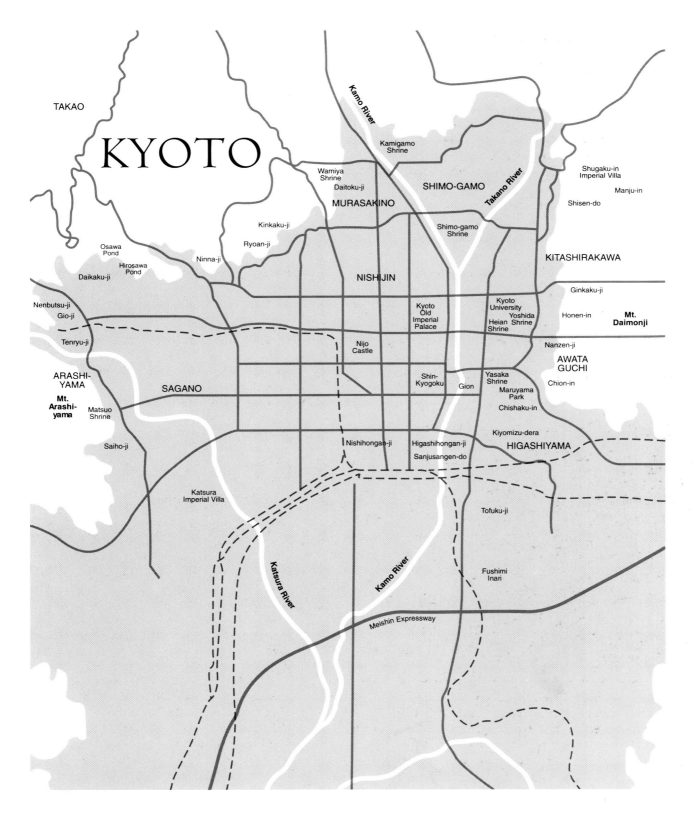

KYOTO

TAKAO

Kamo River

Kamigamo
Shrine

Wamiya
Shrine

Daitoku-ji

SHIMO-GAMO

Takano River

Shugaku-in
Imperial Villa

Manju-in

MURASAKINO

Shisen-do

Kinkaku-ji

Shimo-gamo
Shrine

Osawa
Pond

Ryoan-ji

KITASHIRAKAWA

Hirosawa
Pond

Ninna-ji

NISHIJIN

Ginkaku-ji

Daikaku-ji

Nenbutsu-ji

Kyoto
Old
Imperial
Palace

Kyoto
University

Gio-ji

Honen-in

Mt.
Daimonji

Yoshida
Shrine

Heian
Shrine

Tenryu-ji

Nijo
Castle

Nanzen-ji

ARASHI-
YAMA

AWATA
GUCHI

Mt.
Arashi-
yama

SAGANO

Shin-
Kyogoku

Yasaka
Shrine

Chion-in

Matsuo
Shrine

Gion

Maruyama
Park

Saiho-ji

Chishaku-in

Kiyomizu-dera

Nishihongan-ji

Higashihongan-ji

HIGASHIYAMA

Sanjusangen-do

Katsura
Imperial Villa

Tofuku-ji

Katsura River

Kamo River

Fushimi
Inari

Meishin Expressway

WORDS FOR SHOPKEEPERS TO LIVE BY

As in every culture, Japan has countless proverbs and old sayings handed down by ancestors who learned life's lessons the hard way and hoped to save their progeny trouble by sharing whatever wisdom they had gleaned. In Kyoto, particularly, where people are accustomed to doing things the same way they have always been done, both merchants and their customers are very set in their ways—and have a fine set of proverbs and sayings to reinforce their convictions.

"AKINAI WA USHI NO YODARE"—"Business is like cow spittle." A successful commercial undertaking, if it is to be of enduring value, must be as cohesive and tenacious, as persistent and unbreakable as the drool of a cow. Anyone who has owned a reputable business (or been licked by an affectionate cow) knows this to be true. Those who have not must take my word for it, and the word of most old Kyoto merchants.

"AKINDO NI KEIZU NASHI"—"A merchant has no family tree." Puzzling, when you consider how much pride Kyoto merchants take in their long family heritage, but not when you realize what the saying is getting at. In short, a good family name is not enough to maintain a reputation in Kyoto; no matter how great a shop-

keeper or craftsman your father might have been, your business will collapse if you cannot maintain the high standards he set, and the ones his father set before him.

"OKYAKUSAN WA KAMISAMA," meaning "The customer is god," is similar to sayings in many cultures, but in Kyoto it has a double meaning. Not only should customers be treated as honored guests (because theirs is the hand that feeds you), but due respect should also be accorded to the power of life and death they hold over your shop's good name. Many a Kyoto shop has met its fate through the shopkeeper's most dreaded curse—the gossip of a dissatisfied customer.

"AKINDO WA SONSHITE ITSUKA KURA GA TATSU"—"Even while a shopkeeper stands out front complaining about how bad business is, out back they're busy building him a new storehouse." Kyoto merchants are notorious for saying the opposite of what they really mean, a habit of caution that perhaps originated in the old days when the city was at the mercy of warring clans, and when to let it be known whose side you were really on often resulted in loss of your business, not to mention your head. Added to that is the traditional Japanese belief that it is unwise, unbecoming, and generally in bad taste to flaunt your wealth. Just a year after Louis XIV completed his bombastic palace at Versailles in 1682, Emperor Go-Mino took up residence at Shugaku-in, a comparatively modest villa amid the rice fields of northeastern Kyoto. A more vivid contrast in cultural expressions of wealth would be hard to find. For the merchants too, it was a case of the quieter the better—though perhaps this had more to do with fooling the taxman than simple good manners. Perhaps East and West do have a few things in common after all?

KYOTO DIALECT

The Gentler Tones of the Ancient Capital

As I pass through the streets of this city at night, I look at them as I would at a beloved person. Every city has its sex...this one is all female.
    Nikos Kazantzakis, 1963

At last a notion on which East and West can agree. Kyoto, the lady, speaks in a soft, well-mannered voice (unless you happen to catch an aggrieved *o-basan* on a particularly hectic day). The Kyoto dialect has no rough edges, especially on the practiced tongue of a geisha in Gion: whether she be eighteen or eighty-one, lilting tones and polite phrases powder her every word a gentle pink.

Ever since television brought "standard" (Tokyo) Japanese into every noodle shop and living room in the country, the Kyoto dialect has been suffering a decline. Now spoken primarily in the geisha quarters and by older women, it apparently still comes in handy whenever a difficult situation requires an inscrutable turn of phrase or two (for which *Kyoto-ben*, as it is called, is made to order). People from other parts of Japan say that Kyoto people are the most difficult to deal with—intentionally vague and circumspect, they often say the opposite of what they mean. Polite to a fault, the Japanese, in the words of Paul Theroux, "have perfected good manners and made them indistinguishable from rudeness." Indeed, one of the ways to express anger in Kyoto is to assume an exceptionally polite manner with a close friend. Here are a few Kyoto-isms with which to begin unraveling the puzzle:

"OIDEYASU!" (or *"OKOSHIYASU!"*)—The first word you're likely to hear in an old Kyoto shop. It means simply "welcome" or "please come in" (*"Irasshaimase"* in standard Japanese). The *-yasu* ending is a Kyoto dialect verb ending used to soften the phrase.

"OKINI!"—Thank you "in a big way" is used only in the Kansai district and will almost always win the foreigner who uses it an incredulous smile in Kyoto. Novices are only expected to know the *arigato* of standard Japanese.

"JUNSAI"—Literally, a slimy fungus that grows in Midoriga-ike Pond in Kyoto; figuratively used to describe a person of equally slippery character. "*Ano hito wa junsai na hito ya wa!*"—"He's a very slippery

character, you know!" The expression is used to refer to a glib, outgoing person who never says what he really thinks, but is very charming while he avoids saying it.

"HANNARI SHITA"—To say something or someone is *hannari shita* is to pay them a very Kyoto-style compliment. If something is rich in color, but not gaudy; charming, but not overbearing; elegant, but not showy—it is *hannari shita*.

"KANGAE SASETOKURI-YASU"—"*Kangae-sasete kudasai,*" in standard Japanese, literally meaning "Please allow me to think it over," means "No way" in Kyoto, where it is more polite to evade the question than to give a negative answer.

"OCHAZUKE DEMO DODOSU"—"How about staying for a bite to eat?" in Kyoto informs the visitor that it is time for him to go home. Notorious for saying the opposite of what they mean (a veritable hell for students of beginning Japanese), Kyoto people seldom need to use this phrase, except when dealing with outsiders, because none of their friends would ever dream of staying past the appropriate time.

What's in a word? Sometimes the keys to a city...

LIST OF SHOPS

AIZEN KOBO *indigo textiles*
Omiya Nishi-iru, Nakasuji-dori,
Kamigyo-ku
TEL. (075) 441–0355
(English spoken)
OPEN: Daily, 9 A.M.–5:30 P.M.

AZEKURA *soba noodles*
30 Okamoto-cho, Kamigamo,
Kita-ku
TEL. (075) 701–0161
OPEN: 9 A.M.–5 P.M.
CLOSED: Mondays
PRICES: from ¥600

BUNNOSUKE-JAYA *amazake*
Kodaiji-mon-mae, Higashiyama-ku
TEL. (075) 551–1376
OPEN: 10 A.M.–6 P.M.
CLOSED: Wednesdays
PRICES: ¥390–¥670

FUKA *fu (wheat gluten)*
Sawaragi-cho-agaru,
Nishi-no-Toin-dori, Kamigyo-ku
TEL. (075) 231–1584
OPEN: 9 A.M.–5 P.M.
CLOSED: Wednesdays and
last Sunday

GEKKEIKAN *saké brewery*
247 Minamihama-cho, Fushimi-ku
TEL. (075) 623-2000 (Reception),
623-2105 (Publicity)
OPEN: Showroom and museum,
9:00 A.M.–4:30 P.M.
CLOSED: Mondays

HEIHACHI-JAYA *inn, restaurant*
8-1 Kawagishi-cho,
Yamabana, Sakyo-ku
TEL. (075) 781–5008
CHECK-IN: 4 P.M.
CHECK-OUT: 10 A.M.
CLOSED: 4th Wednesday
RATES: ¥25,000 (w/ 2 meals);
bath only, ¥1,000 plus ¥400
(for use of *yukata*)
RESTAURANT OPEN:
11 A.M.–9 P.M. (seating until 7 P.M.)
CLOSED: 4th Wednesday
PRICES: lunch from ¥3,000,
dinner from ¥10,000

HIIRAGI-YA *inn*
Oike-kado, Fuya-cho-dori,
Nakagyo-ku
TEL. (075) 221–1136
(English spoken)
CHECK-IN: 3 P.M.
CHECK-OUT: 11 A.M.
RATES: ¥30,000–¥90,000

HIRANO-YA *ayu (sweet fish)*
16 Senno-cho, Saga Toriimoto,
Ukyo-ku
TEL. (075) 861–0359
OPEN: Daily, 11:30 A.M.–9 P.M.
PRICES: ¥5,000–¥20,000

HIRATA *blinds*
Shijo-agaru, Yamato Oji-dori,
Higashiyama-ku
TEL. (075) 561-1776
OPEN: Daily, 9:30 A.M.–6:30 P.M.
CLOSED: Sundays, holidays
PRICES: from ¥2,500

ICHIWA *rice cakes*
69 Imamiya-cho, Murasakino,
Kita-ku
TEL. (075) 492–6852
OPEN: 10 A.M.–5 P.M.
CLOSED: Wednesdays
PRICES: from ¥500

IPPODO *tea*
Nijo-kita, Teramachi-dori,
Nakagyo-ku
TEL. (075) 211–3421
(English spoken)
OPEN: 9 A.M.–7 P.M.
CLOSED: Sundays, holidays

IRIYAMA TOFU *tofu*
Aburanokoji-Kado, Sawaragi-cho,
Kamigyo-ku
TEL. (075) 241–2339
OPEN: from 10 A.M. until 5 P.M.
CLOSED: Sundays

JUSAN-YA *combs*
Otabi-cho, Shin-kyogoku
Higashi-iru, Shijo-dori,
Shimogyo-ku
TEL. (075) 211-0498
OPEN: Daily, 11 A.M.–8:30 P.M.

KAGOSHIN *bamboo*
Shichi-ken-cho, Ohashi-higashi
4-chome, Sanjo-dori
TEL. (075) 771–0209, 751–0701
OPEN: Daily, 9 A.M.–7:30 P.M.

KASAGI-YA *sweets & tea*
349 Masuya-cho, Kodai-ji,
Higashiyama-ku
TEL. (075) 561–9562
OPEN: 11 A.M.–6 P.M.
(7 P.M. June–Sept.)
CLOSED: Tuesdays
PRICES: from ¥500

KIKAKU-TEI *inn, restaurant*
55 Higashi-yama-cho,
Kamitakano, Sakyo-ku
TEL. (075) 781–4001
CHECK-IN: 4 P.M.
CHECK-OUT: 10 A.M.
RATES: from ¥20,000
(w/ 2 meals)
RESTAURANT OPEN:
Lunch only, 12–2:30
(reservations required)
CLOSED: 2 days a month
PRICES: from ¥10,000

KINMATA *inn, restaurant*
407 Shijo-agaru, Goko-machi,
Nakagyo-ku
TEL. (075) 221–1039
(English spoken)
CHECK-IN: 3 P.M.
CHECK-OUT: 10 A.M.
RATES: ¥12,000 (room only), ¥15,000
(w/ breakfast), f
rom ¥25,000 (w/ 2 meals)
(reservations required)
RESTAURANT OPEN:
12 A.M.–1 P.M. (last seating),
5:30 P.M.–7 P.M. (last seating)
(reservations required at least one day
in advance)
PRICES: mini-*kaiseki* lunch from
¥4,000, *kaiseki* dinner from ¥10,000

MINOKO *cha-kaiseki cuisine*
480 Kiyoi-cho, Shimogawara-dori,
Gion, Higashiyama-ku
TEL. (075) 561–0328
OPEN: 11:30 A.M.–2:30 P.M.
6 P.M.–8 P.M.(last order, 8 P.M.)
CLOSED: periodically
PRICES: *bento* lunch from ¥4,500,
kaiseki lunch from ¥10,000,
kaiseki dinner from ¥13,000.

MISOKA-AN KAWAMICHIYA
soba noodles
Sanjo-agaru, Fuya-cho-dori,
Nakagyo-ku
TEL. (075) 221–2525,
231-8507 (English spoken)
OPEN: 11 A.M.–8 P.M.
CLOSED: some Thursdays
PRICES: ¥1,000–¥3,500

MIYAWAKI BAISEN-AN *fans*
Tominokoji Nishi-iru, Rokkaku-dori,
Nakagyo-ku
TEL. (075) 221–0181
OPEN: 9 A.M.–6 P.M.
CLOSED: periodically

MORITA WAGAMI
handmade paper
Bukko-ji-agaru, Higashino-toin-dori,
Shimogyo-ku
TEL. (075) 341–0123
OPEN: 9:45 A.M.–5:30 P.M.
Saturday: 9:45 A.M.–4:30 P.M.
CLOSED: 1st day of each month,
Sundays, holidays

MURAKAMI-JU *pickles*
Shijo-sagaru, Nishi-Kiyamachi-dori,
Shimogyo-ku
TEL. (075) 351–1737
OPEN: 9 A.M.–7 P.M. Saturday, Sunday,
holidays open until 7:30 P.M.
CLOSED: 1st & 3rd Wednesdays

NAITO *brooms and brushes*
Sanjo-ohashi Nishi-zume, Nakagyo-ku
TEL. (075) 221–3018
OPEN: Daily, 9 A.M.–7 P.M.

NAKAMURA-RO *restaurant*
Yasaka-jinja-uchi, Gion,
Higashiyama-ku
TEL. (075) 561–0016-8

OPEN: 11:30 A.M.–7 P.M.
(last order, 6 P.M.)
CLOSED: last Thursday
PRICE: lunch from ¥3,500,
dinner (*kaiseki*) from ¥15,000

NAKANISHI TOKU SHOTEN
antique dolls
359 Moto-cho,
Yamato-oji Higashi-iru,
Furumonzen-dori, Higashiyama-ku
TEL. (075) 561–7309
OPEN: 10 A.M.–6 P.M.
CLOSED: periodically

NARITA *pickles*
35 Yamamoto-cho, Kamigamo, Kita-ku
TEL. (075) 721–1567
OPEN: 10 A.M.–6 P.M.
CLOSED: Wednesdays

NISHIKI *kaiseki cuisine*
Nakanoshima-koen-uchi, Arashiyama,
Ukyo-ku
TEL. (075) 871–8888, 881–8888
OPEN: 11 A.M.–7:30 P.M.
CLOSED: Tuesdays
PRICES: from ¥3,800 (tables)
and ¥6,000 (tatami).

NISHIHARU *woodblock prints*
Teramachi-kado, Sanjo-dori,
Nakagyo-ku
TEL. (075) 211–2849
(English spoken)
OPEN: Daily, 2 P.M.–8 P.M.

SAIUNDO
Japanese-painting supplies
Fuya-cho Higashi-iru, Anekoji,
Nakagyo-ku
TEL. (075) 221–2464
(English spoken)
OPEN: 9 A.M.–6 P.M.
CLOSED: 1st & 3rd Wednesdays

SHIOYOSHI-KEN
Kyoto confectionery
Nakadachi-uri-agaru, Kuromon-dori,
Kamigyo-ku
TEL. (075) 441–0803
OPEN: 9 A.M.–6 P.M.
CLOSED: Sundays, holidays,
third Wednesday

SHOYEIDO *incense*
Nijo-agaru, Karasuma-dori,
Nakagyo-ku
TEL. (075) 231–2307
OPEN: Daily 8:30 A.M.–5:30 P.M.
(Saturdays, Sundays, holidays
open from 9 A.M.)

TAKASEBUNE *tempura*
188 Sendo-cho, Shijo-sagaru,
Shimogyo-ku
TEL. (075) 351–4032
OPEN: 11 A.M.–3 P.M.,
4:30 P.M.–9:30 P.M.
CLOSED: Mondays
PRICES: ¥700–¥3,200

TARUDEN *buckets*
332 Higashi Yashiro-cho, Omiya
Nishi-iru Rosan-ji-dori, Kamigyo-ku
TEL. (075) 431–3087
OPEN: Daily, 8 A.M.–8 P.M.

TAWARA-YA *inn*
Anekoji-agaru, Fuya-cho-dori,
Nakagyo-ku
TEL. (075) 211–5566
(English spoken)
CHECK-IN: 1 P.M.
CHECK-OUT: 11 A.M.
RATES: ¥33,000–¥75,000

TSUKIMOCHI-YA NAOMASA
Kyoto confectionery
Sanjo-agaru, Hachi-ken-me,
Kiyamachi-dori, Nakagyo-ku
TEL. (075) 231–0175
OPEN: 9 A.M.–8 P.M.
CLOSED: Thursdays,
some Wednesdays

YAMATO MINGEI *folk art*
Tako-yakushi-agaru, Kawara-machi,
Nakagyo-ku
TEL. (075) 221–2641
OPEN: 10 A.M.–8:30 P.M.
CLOSED: Tuesdays

YUBAHAN *yuba*
(*soy milk "skins"*)
Oike-agaru, Fuya-cho-dori,
Nakagyo-ku
TEL. (075) 221–5622
OPEN: 7 A.M.–6 P.M.
CLOSED: Thursdays

Suggested Reading List

Mosher, Gouverneur.
Kyoto: A Contemplative Guide.
Tokyo: Tuttle, 1978.

Plutchow, Herbert E.
Historical Kyoto.
Tokyo: Japan Times, 1983.

Ponsonby-Fane, R.
Kyoto: The Old Capital of Japan (794–1869).
Tokyo: Ponsonby Memorial Society, 1956.

Sansom, George.
A Short Cultural History of Japan.
Tokyo: Tuttle, 1981.

Steward, Harold.
By the Old Walls of Kyoto.
Tokyo: Weatherhill, 1981.

Tanizaki Jun'ichiro.
In Praise of Shadows.
Branford, Conn.: Leete's Island Books, 1977.
Reprint, Tokyo: Tuttle, 1984.

Treib, Mark and Ronald Herman.
A Guide to the Gardens of Kyoto.
Tokyo: Shufunotomo, 1983.

ACKNOWLEDGMENTS

I would like to express my deepest thanks, first of all, to Yoko Yoshikawa Couling, whose help was invaluable to me from the days when this book was just another crazy idea. Without her capable assistance and support this book would still be in the crazy idea basket.

Thanks also to Rieko Iwaki, Mikiko Murata, and Mayumi Mizuguchi for their assistance; to those who gave away their favorite (and occasionally secret) shops, especially to Philip Meredith and Joseph Justice (who dragged me all over Muromachi in search of the roots of *Kyo-ryori*, a cuisine at which he has become an artist); to Kenkichi and Aiko Kuroda, Toshitaka Kawai, Hirotoshi Kuwano, and Kazuko Saito, who taught me how to think Japanese; to Claire Gallian, who made sure I got my *daidoko* and *toriniwa* in the right places; and to Yasuo Kitazawa, for introducing me to the world of Kyoto crafts.

Many thanks to Lucy Birmingham Fujii, whose beautiful pictures tell more than my words; and to the Kyoto Chamber of Commerce and Industry for permission to reprint old photographs of Kyoto from their collection.

Thank you always, Donald Richie, for your friendship, moral support, and advice—to Lisa Oyama, Hiroshi Kagawa, and Jules Young at Kodansha International for building something liveable out of rough timbers and dangling participles; to David Jack and the staff of the *Kansai Time Out*, in which my "Oideyasu" series on old Kyoto shops first appeared; to Tom Chapman and Greg Starr for publishing a portion of the material in this book in a different form in *Winds*; to Margaret O'Sullivan, for reading valiantly through the raggedy new parts … thank you. Thanks also to Robert Singer for his expertise and editorial advice. Special thanks to Barry Lancet, K.I. editor of this new edition—without his support it would never have come to be. And first, last, and always—to my husband, Stephen Futscher, whose belief in me has helped me to believe in myself.